50 German Cake Recipes for Home

By: Kelly Johnson

Table of Contents

- Black Forest Cake (Schwarzwälder Kirschtorte)
- Bee Sting Cake (Bienenstich)
- German Apple Cake (Apfelkuchen)
- Streuselkuchen (Crumb Cake)
- Sacher Torte
- Linzer Torte
- Frankfurter Kranz
- Donauwelle (Danube Wave Cake)
- Zwetschgenkuchen (Plum Cake)
- German Chocolate Cake (Deutsche Schokoladentorte)
- Eierschecke (Dresden Egg Custard Cake)
- Stollen
- Baumkuchen (Tree Cake)
- Mohnkuchen (Poppy Seed Cake)
- Quarkstollen (Quark-filled Stollen)
- Rote Grütze Torte (Red Berry Pudding Cake)
- Käsekuchen (German Cheesecake)
- Nusstorte (Nut Cake)
- Erdbeerkuchen (Strawberry Cake)
- Russischer Zupfkuchen (Russian Cheesecake Brownie)
- Mohrenkopftorte (Chocolate Marshmallow Cake)
- Apfelstrudel (Apple Strudel)
- Himbeertorte (Raspberry Cake)
- Pflaumenmus Kuchen (Plum Butter Cake)
- Prinzregententorte
- Windbeutel (Cream Puff Cake)
- Schnecken (Cinnamon Rolls)
- Dampfnudeln (Steamed Dumplings)
- Berliner Pfannkuchen (Berlin Pancakes)
- Streuselplätzchen (Streusel Cookies)
- Lebkuchen (German Gingerbread)
- Marzipan Kartoffeln (Marzipan Potatoes)
- Eiskaffee Torte (Iced Coffee Cake)
- Gugelhupf (Bundt Cake)
- Kartoffelkuchen (Potato Cake)

- Rhabarberkuchen (Rhubarb Cake)
- Butterkuchen (Butter Cake)
- Spaghettieis Torte (Spaghetti Ice Cream Cake)
- Holunderblütenkuchen (Elderflower Cake)
- Kalter Hund (No-Bake Chocolate Biscuit Cake)
- Sonntagskuchen (Sunday Cake)
- Zitronenkuchen (Lemon Cake)
- Schmandkuchen (Sour Cream Cake)
- Beerenkuchen (Berry Cake)
- Kirschtorte (Cherry Cake)
- Aprikosenkuchen (Apricot Cake)
- Sauerkirsch Streuselkuchen (Sour Cherry Crumb Cake)
- Kirschschnitten (Cherry Slices)
- Schokoladenkuchen (Chocolate Cake)
- Zupfkuchen (German Chocolate Marble Cake)

Black Forest Cake (Schwarzwälder Kirschtorte)

Ingredients:

- Chocolate sponge cake layers: Light and airy chocolate cake layers, often soaked in Kirsch.
- Cherries: Traditionally sour cherries, soaked in Kirsch for flavor and moistness.
- Whipped cream: Sweetened whipped cream is used generously between layers and on top of the cake.
- Kirsch (Kirschwasser): A clear, colorless fruit brandy made from sour cherries, used to enhance the flavor of both the cherries and the cake layers.
- Chocolate shavings or curls: For decoration, often sprinkled on top and sometimes around the sides of the cake.

Assembly:

1. **Cake Layers**: Typically, three layers of chocolate sponge cake are baked and cooled.
2. **Cherries**: The cherries are pitted and soaked in Kirsch, which not only flavors the cherries but also adds moisture to the cake layers.
3. **Whipped Cream**: Each cake layer is sandwiched with whipped cream and cherries. The sides and top of the cake are covered generously with whipped cream.
4. **Decoration**: Finally, the cake is decorated with chocolate shavings or curls on top. Sometimes, additional cherries are used as garnish.

The combination of chocolate, cherries, cream, and a hint of Kirsch gives the Black Forest Cake its distinctive flavor profile. It's a decadent dessert enjoyed for special occasions and celebrations, both in Germany and around the world.

Bee Sting Cake (Bienenstich)

Ingredients:

For the Yeast Dough:

- 2 cups (250g) all-purpose flour
- 2 1/4 teaspoons (7g or 1 packet) active dry yeast
- 1/4 cup (50g) granulated sugar
- 1/2 teaspoon salt
- 1/2 cup (120ml) milk
- 1/4 cup (60g) unsalted butter, softened
- 2 large eggs

For the Vanilla Custard Filling:

- 2 cups (480ml) milk
- 1/2 cup (100g) granulated sugar
- 1/4 cup (30g) cornstarch
- 2 large egg yolks
- 1 teaspoon vanilla extract

For the Almond Topping:

- 1/2 cup (100g) unsalted butter
- 1/2 cup (100g) granulated sugar
- 2 tablespoons honey
- 1 1/2 cups (150g) sliced almonds

Instructions:

1. Make the Yeast Dough:

- In a large mixing bowl, combine flour, yeast, sugar, and salt.
- In a small saucepan, heat the milk and butter until warm (about 110-115°F or 45-50°C), stirring until the butter melts.
- Pour the warm milk mixture into the flour mixture and stir until combined.
- Add eggs, one at a time, mixing well after each addition.
- Knead the dough on a lightly floured surface for about 5-7 minutes until smooth and elastic.
- Place the dough in a greased bowl, cover with a clean kitchen towel or plastic wrap, and let it rise in a warm place until doubled in size, about 1-2 hours.

2. Prepare the Vanilla Custard Filling:

- In a medium saucepan, heat the milk until steaming, but not boiling.

- In a separate bowl, whisk together sugar, cornstarch, and egg yolks until smooth.
- Gradually pour the hot milk into the sugar mixture, whisking constantly.
- Return the mixture to the saucepan and cook over medium heat, stirring constantly, until thickened and bubbling.
- Remove from heat and stir in vanilla extract.
- Transfer the custard to a bowl, cover with plastic wrap directly on the surface to prevent a skin from forming, and refrigerate until chilled and thickened.

3. Make the Almond Topping:

- In a saucepan, melt butter, sugar, and honey over medium heat, stirring until sugar dissolves.
- Stir in almonds and cook for 2-3 minutes until the mixture is slightly thickened and golden.
- Remove from heat and let cool slightly.

4. Assemble and Bake:

- Preheat your oven to 350°F (175°C). Grease and line a 9-inch round cake pan with parchment paper.
- Punch down the risen dough and transfer it to the prepared pan, pressing it evenly to cover the bottom.
- Spread the chilled custard evenly over the dough.
- Evenly distribute the almond topping over the custard layer.
- Bake for 25-30 minutes, or until the top is golden brown and the dough is cooked through.
- Remove from the oven and let cool in the pan for 10 minutes before transferring to a wire rack to cool completely.

5. Serve:

- Once cooled, slice and serve the Bee Sting Cake. Enjoy the delicious combination of soft, yeasty dough, creamy vanilla custard, and crunchy caramelized almonds!

This recipe captures the essence of the traditional German Bee Sting Cake, perfect for sharing with friends and family. Enjoy baking!

German Apple Cake (Apfelkuchen)

Ingredients:

For the Cake:

- 1 1/2 cups (190g) all-purpose flour
- 1 1/2 teaspoons baking powder
- 1/2 teaspoon salt
- 1/2 cup (115g) unsalted butter, softened
- 3/4 cup (150g) granulated sugar
- 2 large eggs
- 1 teaspoon vanilla extract
- 1/4 cup (60ml) milk

For the Apple Topping:

- 3-4 medium apples (such as Granny Smith or Braeburn), peeled, cored, and thinly sliced
- 2 tablespoons granulated sugar
- 1 teaspoon ground cinnamon

Optional Topping:

- Powdered sugar, for dusting

Instructions:

1. Preheat Oven and Prepare Pan:

- Preheat your oven to 350°F (175°C). Grease and flour a 9-inch round cake pan or line it with parchment paper for easy removal.

2. Make the Cake Batter:

- In a medium bowl, whisk together flour, baking powder, and salt. Set aside.
- In a large mixing bowl, cream together softened butter and sugar until light and fluffy.
- Beat in eggs, one at a time, until well combined. Stir in vanilla extract.
- Gradually add the flour mixture to the wet ingredients, alternating with milk, beginning and ending with the flour mixture. Mix until just combined.

3. Prepare the Apple Topping:

- In a small bowl, toss the sliced apples with sugar and cinnamon until evenly coated.

4. Assemble and Bake:

- Spread the cake batter evenly into the prepared cake pan.

- Arrange the sliced apples in overlapping circles on top of the batter.
- Sprinkle any remaining sugar-cinnamon mixture over the apples.

5. Bake:

- Bake in the preheated oven for 40-45 minutes, or until the cake is golden brown and a toothpick inserted into the center comes out clean.

6. Cool and Serve:

- Allow the cake to cool in the pan for 10 minutes before transferring it to a wire rack to cool completely.
- Once cooled, dust with powdered sugar if desired.
- Slice and serve the German Apple Cake warm or at room temperature.

Tips:

- You can enhance the flavor by adding a tablespoon of rum or lemon zest to the apple slices before arranging them on the cake.
- Serve with a dollop of whipped cream or a scoop of vanilla ice cream for an extra treat.

This Apfelkuchen recipe is perfect for enjoying the flavors of fresh apples in a comforting, homemade cake. Enjoy baking and savoring this traditional German dessert!

Streuselkuchen (Crumb Cake)

Ingredients:

For the Cake:

- 2 cups (250g) all-purpose flour
- 1/2 cup (100g) granulated sugar
- 1 teaspoon baking powder
- 1/4 teaspoon salt
- 1/2 cup (115g) unsalted butter, cold and cut into small pieces
- 1 large egg
- 1 teaspoon vanilla extract
- 1/2 cup (120ml) milk

For the Streusel Topping:

- 1 cup (125g) all-purpose flour
- 1/2 cup (100g) granulated sugar
- 1/2 cup (115g) unsalted butter, cold and cut into small pieces
- 1 teaspoon ground cinnamon

Optional Glaze:

- 1/2 cup (60g) powdered sugar
- 1-2 tablespoons milk or water

Instructions:

1. Preheat Oven and Prepare Pan:

- Preheat your oven to 350°F (175°C). Grease and flour a 9x13-inch baking dish or line it with parchment paper for easy removal.

2. Make the Streusel Topping:

- In a medium bowl, combine flour, sugar, and cinnamon.
- Cut in the cold butter using a pastry cutter or your fingers until the mixture resembles coarse crumbs. Set aside.

3. Make the Cake Batter:

- In a large mixing bowl, whisk together flour, sugar, baking powder, and salt.
- Cut in the cold butter until the mixture resembles coarse crumbs.
- In a separate bowl, whisk together the egg, vanilla extract, and milk.
- Gradually add the wet ingredients to the dry ingredients, mixing until just combined and no large lumps remain. The batter will be thick.

4. Assemble and Bake:

- Spread the cake batter evenly into the prepared baking dish, smoothing the top with a spatula.
- Sprinkle the streusel topping evenly over the cake batter, covering it completely.

5. Bake:

- Bake in the preheated oven for 30-35 minutes, or until the streusel topping is golden brown and a toothpick inserted into the center of the cake comes out clean.

6. Optional Glaze:

- If desired, whisk together powdered sugar and milk or water until smooth. Drizzle the glaze over the warm Streuselkuchen.

7. Cool and Serve:

- Allow the cake to cool in the pan on a wire rack for at least 20-30 minutes before slicing and serving.

Tips:

- Serve Streuselkuchen warm or at room temperature with a cup of coffee or tea.
- Store any leftovers in an airtight container at room temperature for up to 3 days.

Enjoy this classic German Streuselkuchen, perfect for breakfast, brunch, or as a delightful afternoon treat!

Sacher Torte

Ingredients:

For the Cake:

- 7 ounces (200g) dark chocolate (around 70% cocoa), chopped
- 7 tablespoons (100g) unsalted butter, softened
- 3/4 cup (150g) granulated sugar
- 6 large eggs, separated
- 1/2 cup (60g) ground almonds or hazelnuts
- 1/2 cup (60g) all-purpose flour

For the Apricot Jam Filling:

- 1 cup (250g) apricot jam

For the Chocolate Glaze:

- 7 ounces (200g) dark chocolate (around 70% cocoa), chopped
- 1/2 cup (120ml) heavy cream
- 2 tablespoons (30g) unsalted butter

Instructions:

1. Prepare the Cake:

- Preheat your oven to 350°F (175°C). Grease and line the bottom of a 9-inch (23cm) round cake pan with parchment paper.
- Melt the chopped chocolate in a heatproof bowl over a pot of simmering water (double boiler method), stirring until smooth. Let it cool slightly.
- In a large mixing bowl, cream together the softened butter and sugar until pale and fluffy.
- Add the egg yolks one at a time, mixing well after each addition.
- Mix in the melted chocolate, ground almonds or hazelnuts, and flour until well combined.
- In a separate bowl, whip the egg whites until stiff peaks form. Gently fold the whipped egg whites into the chocolate batter in three additions, being careful not to deflate the mixture.
- Pour the batter into the prepared cake pan and smooth the top with a spatula.
- Bake for about 35-40 minutes, or until a toothpick inserted into the center comes out clean.
- Let the cake cool in the pan for 10 minutes, then transfer it to a wire rack to cool completely.

2. Prepare the Apricot Jam Filling:

- While the cake is cooling, heat the apricot jam in a small saucepan over low heat until it becomes smooth and spreadable. Set aside to cool slightly.

3. Assemble the Sacher Torte:

- Once the cake has cooled completely, carefully slice it horizontally into two even layers.
- Spread a generous layer of apricot jam over the top of one cake layer, then place the other layer on top, sandwiching them together.

4. Make the Chocolate Glaze:

- In a heatproof bowl, combine the chopped chocolate and butter.
- In a small saucepan, heat the heavy cream until it just begins to simmer. Pour the hot cream over the chocolate and butter mixture. Let it sit for 2-3 minutes, then stir until smooth and glossy.

5. Glaze the Cake:

- Place the assembled cake on a wire rack set over a baking sheet or parchment paper (to catch drips).
- Pour the warm chocolate glaze over the top of the cake, spreading it evenly with a spatula to cover the top and sides.

6. Chill and Serve:

- Allow the glaze to set at room temperature for at least 1 hour, or refrigerate for 30 minutes, until firm.
- Slice the Sacher Torte using a sharp knife dipped in hot water for clean cuts.

7. Serve:

- Serve slices of Sacher Torte at room temperature, garnished with whipped cream if desired.

Enjoy this rich and elegant Sacher Torte, a true classic in European pastry traditions!

Linzer Torte

Ingredients:

For the Dough:

- 1 1/2 cups (190g) all-purpose flour
- 1 cup (100g) ground almonds or hazelnuts
- 1/2 teaspoon ground cinnamon
- 1/4 teaspoon ground cloves
- 1/4 teaspoon salt
- 3/4 cup (170g) unsalted butter, softened
- 3/4 cup (150g) granulated sugar
- 1 large egg
- 1 teaspoon vanilla extract
- Zest of 1 lemon

For the Filling:

- 1 cup (250g) raspberry jam or any preferred fruit preserves

For Dusting:

- Confectioners' sugar, for dusting

Instructions:

1. Prepare the Dough:

- In a medium bowl, whisk together flour, ground almonds or hazelnuts, cinnamon, cloves, and salt. Set aside.
- In a large mixing bowl, cream together softened butter and sugar until light and fluffy.
- Add the egg, vanilla extract, and lemon zest to the butter mixture, and beat until well combined.
- Gradually add the flour mixture to the wet ingredients, mixing until the dough comes together. It will be slightly crumbly but should hold together when pressed.
- Divide the dough into two portions, one slightly larger than the other. Flatten each portion into a disc, wrap them separately in plastic wrap, and refrigerate for at least 1 hour or until firm.

2. Preheat Oven and Prepare Pan:

- Preheat your oven to 350°F (175°C). Grease a 9-inch (23cm) round tart pan with removable bottom, or a similar-sized cake pan.

3. Roll Out the Dough:

- On a lightly floured surface, roll out the larger portion of dough to about 1/4-inch (6mm) thickness. Transfer it to the prepared pan, pressing it gently into the bottom and up the sides. Trim any excess dough if necessary.

4. Add the Filling:

- Spread the raspberry jam evenly over the dough in the pan.

5. Form the Lattice Top:

- Roll out the remaining dough to the same thickness. Using a sharp knife or a fluted pastry wheel, cut the dough into strips (about 1/2 inch wide).
- Arrange the strips in a lattice pattern over the jam-filled dough, pressing the ends gently to seal them to the edges of the crust.

6. Bake:

- Bake in the preheated oven for 30-35 minutes, or until the crust is golden brown.

7. Cool and Serve:

- Allow the Linzer Torte to cool in the pan for about 10 minutes before transferring it to a wire rack to cool completely.
- Once cooled, dust with confectioners' sugar before serving.

8. Serve:

- Slice and serve the Linzer Torte at room temperature. It pairs wonderfully with coffee or tea.

Enjoy this classic Linzer Torte with its beautiful lattice design and delicious raspberry jam filling, perfect for any occasion!

Frankfurter Kranz

Ingredients:

For the Cake:

- 2 cups (250g) all-purpose flour
- 2 teaspoons baking powder
- 1/4 teaspoon salt
- 1 cup (225g) unsalted butter, softened
- 1 cup (200g) granulated sugar
- 1 teaspoon vanilla extract
- 4 large eggs
- 1/4 cup (60ml) milk

For the Buttercream Filling:

- 1 cup (225g) unsalted butter, softened
- 2 cups (250g) powdered sugar
- 2 teaspoons vanilla extract
- 1/2 cup (125g) raspberry or strawberry jam (optional, for filling)

For the Caramelized Nut Topping:

- 1 cup (125g) chopped nuts (traditionally hazelnuts or almonds)
- 1/2 cup (100g) granulated sugar
- 2 tablespoons water

Instructions:

1. Prepare the Cake:

- Preheat your oven to 350°F (175°C). Grease and flour two 8-inch (20cm) round cake pans.
- In a medium bowl, whisk together flour, baking powder, and salt. Set aside.
- In a large mixing bowl, cream together softened butter, sugar, and vanilla extract until light and fluffy.
- Add eggs one at a time, beating well after each addition.
- Gradually add the flour mixture to the wet ingredients, alternating with the milk, beginning and ending with the flour mixture. Mix until just combined.
- Divide the batter evenly between the prepared cake pans, smoothing the tops with a spatula.
- Bake for 25-30 minutes, or until a toothpick inserted into the center of the cakes comes out clean.
- Remove from the oven and let the cakes cool in the pans for 10 minutes before transferring them to wire racks to cool completely.

2. Make the Buttercream Filling:

- In a large mixing bowl, beat softened butter until creamy.
- Gradually add powdered sugar, beating until light and fluffy.
- Beat in vanilla extract until well combined.

3. Assemble the Frankfurter Kranz:

- If using jam, spread a layer of jam on the top of one cake layer. Then spread a layer of buttercream over the jam.
- Place the second cake layer on top, sandwiching them together with the filling.

4. Prepare the Caramelized Nut Topping:

- In a skillet or saucepan, heat granulated sugar and water over medium heat until the sugar dissolves, stirring occasionally.
- Once the sugar is dissolved, add the chopped nuts and cook, stirring constantly, until the nuts are caramelized and golden brown.
- Remove from heat and let the caramelized nuts cool and harden slightly.

5. Decorate the Cake:

- Spread a thin layer of buttercream around the sides and top of the assembled cake to create a crumb coat.
- Press the caramelized nuts onto the sides and top of the cake, gently pressing them into the buttercream.
- Transfer any remaining buttercream to a piping bag fitted with a star tip and pipe rosettes or decorative borders around the top edge of the cake.

6. Serve:

- Slice and serve the Frankfurter Kranz at room temperature. It's a delightful treat often enjoyed with coffee or tea.

Enjoy this classic German Frankfurter Kranz, showcasing its rich buttercream filling and crunchy caramelized nut topping!

Donauwelle (Danube Wave Cake)

Ingredients:

For the Cake:

- 1 cup (225g) unsalted butter, softened
- 1 cup (200g) granulated sugar
- 4 large eggs
- 2 cups (250g) all-purpose flour
- 2 teaspoons baking powder
- 1/2 cup (120ml) milk
- 2 tablespoons cocoa powder
- 1 teaspoon vanilla extract

For the Cherry Layer:

- 1 can (about 14 ounces or 400g) pitted sour cherries, drained (reserve juice for soaking)
- 1-2 tablespoons cherry liqueur or cherry juice (reserved from the cherries)

For the Buttercream:

- 1 cup (225g) unsalted butter, softened
- 2 cups (250g) powdered sugar
- 1 teaspoon vanilla extract

For the Chocolate Glaze:

- 7 ounces (200g) dark chocolate, chopped
- 1/2 cup (120ml) heavy cream
- 1 tablespoon unsalted butter

Instructions:

1. Prepare the Cake:

- Preheat your oven to 350°F (175°C). Grease and flour a 9x13-inch (23x33cm) baking dish or line it with parchment paper.
- In a large mixing bowl, cream together softened butter and sugar until light and fluffy.
- Add eggs one at a time, beating well after each addition. Stir in vanilla extract.
- In a separate bowl, whisk together flour and baking powder. Gradually add the flour mixture to the butter mixture, alternating with milk, beginning and ending with the flour mixture. Mix until just combined.
- Divide the batter in half. Stir cocoa powder into one half of the batter until well combined.
- Spread the vanilla batter evenly into the prepared baking dish. Spoon the cocoa batter on top and swirl gently with a knife to create a marbled effect.

- Bake for 25-30 minutes, or until a toothpick inserted into the center comes out clean.
- Remove from the oven and let the cake cool completely in the pan.

2. Prepare the Cherry Layer:

- Drain the sour cherries, reserving the juice. If desired, mix 1-2 tablespoons of cherry liqueur or reserved cherry juice into the cherries for extra flavor.

3. Make the Buttercream:

- In a large mixing bowl, beat softened butter until creamy.
- Gradually add powdered sugar, beating until light and fluffy.
- Beat in vanilla extract until well combined.

4. Assemble the Donauwelle:

- Once the cake has cooled completely, spread a layer of buttercream over the top of the vanilla cake layer.
- Evenly distribute the cherries over the buttercream layer.
- Spread another layer of buttercream over the cherries.

5. Prepare the Chocolate Glaze:

- In a heatproof bowl, combine chopped chocolate, heavy cream, and butter.
- Microwave in 30-second intervals, stirring in between, until the chocolate is melted and the mixture is smooth.

6. Glaze the Cake:

- Pour the warm chocolate glaze over the top of the cake, spreading it evenly with a spatula.

7. Chill and Serve:

- Refrigerate the Donauwelle for at least 1 hour, or until the chocolate glaze is set.
- Slice and serve the Donauwelle at room temperature. Enjoy this delicious German cake with its layers of flavors and textures!

Donauwelle is a wonderful dessert that combines the richness of chocolate and buttercream with the tartness of cherries, making it a favorite for celebrations and gatherings.

Zwetschgenkuchen (Plum Cake)

Ingredients:

For the Dough:

- 1 1/2 cups (190g) all-purpose flour
- 1/2 cup (100g) granulated sugar
- 1 teaspoon baking powder
- 1/4 teaspoon salt
- 1/2 cup (115g) unsalted butter, cold and cut into small pieces
- 1 large egg
- 1 teaspoon vanilla extract

For the Plum Topping:

- 1.5 lbs (700g) plums (Zwetschgen), halved and pitted
- 2 tablespoons granulated sugar
- 1 teaspoon ground cinnamon

For the Streusel Topping (Optional):

- 1/2 cup (65g) all-purpose flour
- 1/4 cup (50g) granulated sugar
- 1/4 cup (55g) unsalted butter, cold and cut into small pieces

Instructions:

1. Prepare the Dough:

- In a large mixing bowl, whisk together flour, sugar, baking powder, and salt.
- Add cold butter pieces and cut into the flour mixture using a pastry cutter or your fingers until it resembles coarse crumbs.
- In a small bowl, whisk together the egg and vanilla extract. Add the egg mixture to the flour mixture and mix until the dough comes together. It will be slightly crumbly but should hold together when pressed.
- Press the dough into the bottom of a greased 9x13-inch (23x33cm) baking dish, forming an even layer. Chill the dough-lined dish in the refrigerator while you prepare the plums.

2. Prepare the Plum Topping:

- Preheat your oven to 375°F (190°C).
- Arrange the halved and pitted plums in a single layer over the chilled dough, cut side up. Press them gently into the dough.
- In a small bowl, mix together granulated sugar and cinnamon. Sprinkle this mixture evenly over the plums.

3. Optional Streusel Topping:

- If using the streusel topping, combine flour and sugar in a bowl. Cut in the cold butter until the mixture resembles coarse crumbs. Sprinkle the streusel evenly over the plums.

4. Bake:

- Bake in the preheated oven for 30-35 minutes, or until the dough is golden brown and the plums are tender.

5. Cool and Serve:

- Let the Zwetschgenkuchen cool slightly in the pan on a wire rack before slicing and serving.
- Serve the plum cake warm or at room temperature. It can be enjoyed plain or with a dollop of whipped cream or a scoop of vanilla ice cream.

Tips:

- Zwetschgen plums are ideal for this cake due to their slightly tart flavor and firm texture when baked. If unavailable, you can use other varieties of plums, adjusting the sugar based on their sweetness.
- This cake is best enjoyed the day it's made but can be stored in an airtight container at room temperature for up to 2 days.

Enjoy this traditional Zwetschgenkuchen, celebrating the sweetness of plums in a simple and delicious cake!

German Chocolate Cake (Deutsche Schokoladentorte)

Ingredients:

For the Chocolate Cake:

- 2 cups (250g) all-purpose flour
- 1 cup (100g) unsweetened cocoa powder
- 2 teaspoons baking powder
- 1 teaspoon baking soda
- 1/2 teaspoon salt
- 1 cup (225g) unsalted butter, softened
- 1 1/2 cups (300g) granulated sugar
- 4 large eggs, room temperature
- 1 cup (240ml) buttermilk, room temperature
- 1/2 cup (120ml) strong brewed coffee, cooled (or water)
- 2 teaspoons vanilla extract

For the Coconut-Pecan Filling:

- 1 cup (240ml) evaporated milk
- 1 cup (200g) granulated sugar
- 3 large egg yolks
- 1/2 cup (115g) unsalted butter, cubed
- 1 teaspoon vanilla extract
- 1 1/3 cups (100g) sweetened shredded coconut
- 1 cup (120g) chopped pecans, toasted

For the Chocolate Ganache Frosting:

- 8 ounces (225g) semi-sweet or dark chocolate, chopped
- 1 cup (240ml) heavy cream
- 2 tablespoons (30g) unsalted butter, softened

Instructions:

1. Prepare the Chocolate Cake:

- Preheat your oven to 350°F (175°C). Grease and flour three 8-inch (20cm) round cake pans, or line them with parchment paper for easy removal.
- In a large bowl, sift together flour, cocoa powder, baking powder, baking soda, and salt. Set aside.
- In another large mixing bowl, cream together softened butter and sugar until light and fluffy.
- Add eggs one at a time, beating well after each addition. Stir in vanilla extract.

- Gradually add the dry ingredients to the butter mixture, alternating with buttermilk and coffee (or water), beginning and ending with the dry ingredients. Mix until just combined.
- Divide the batter evenly among the prepared cake pans, smoothing the tops with a spatula.
- Bake for 25-30 minutes, or until a toothpick inserted into the center of the cakes comes out clean.
- Remove from the oven and let the cakes cool in the pans for 10 minutes before transferring them to wire racks to cool completely.

2. Make the Coconut-Pecan Filling:

- In a medium saucepan, whisk together evaporated milk, sugar, and egg yolks until well combined.
- Add cubed butter and cook over medium heat, stirring constantly, until the mixture thickens (about 10-12 minutes).
- Remove from heat and stir in vanilla extract, shredded coconut, and toasted chopped pecans.
- Let the filling cool to room temperature, stirring occasionally to prevent a skin from forming.

3. Prepare the Chocolate Ganache Frosting:

- Place chopped chocolate in a heatproof bowl.
- In a small saucepan, heat heavy cream over medium heat until it just begins to simmer.
- Pour the hot cream over the chopped chocolate and let it sit for 2-3 minutes. Stir until the chocolate is melted and the mixture is smooth.
- Add softened butter to the ganache and stir until well combined. Let the ganache cool slightly to thicken.

4. Assemble the German Chocolate Cake:

- Place one layer of chocolate cake on a serving platter or cake stand.
- Spread half of the coconut-pecan filling evenly over the top of the cake layer.
- Place the second cake layer on top and spread the remaining filling over it.
- Place the third cake layer on top. Spread a thin layer of chocolate ganache frosting over the top and sides of the cake to crumb coat.
- Chill the cake in the refrigerator for about 15-20 minutes to set the crumb coat.
- Frost the cake with the remaining chocolate ganache, spreading it evenly over the top and sides. You can create decorative swirls or patterns with a spatula or cake comb.

5. Chill and Serve:

- Refrigerate the German Chocolate Cake for at least 1 hour before slicing and serving to allow the ganache to set.
- Slice and serve the cake at room temperature. Enjoy the luxurious flavors of chocolate, coconut, and pecans in every bite!

This German Chocolate Cake is sure to impress with its layers of moist chocolate cake and indulgent filling and frosting. Perfect for celebrations or any special occasion!

Eierschecke (Dresden Egg Custard Cake)

Ingredients:

For the Shortcrust Pastry:

- 1 1/2 cups (190g) all-purpose flour
- 1/2 cup (100g) granulated sugar
- 1/2 teaspoon baking powder
- 1/4 teaspoon salt
- 1/2 cup (115g) unsalted butter, cold and cut into small pieces
- 1 large egg

For the Custard Layer:

- 1 1/2 cups (360ml) milk
- 1/2 cup (100g) granulated sugar
- 1/4 cup (30g) cornstarch
- 1 teaspoon vanilla extract
- 3 large egg yolks

For the Cake Layer:

- 1/2 cup (115g) unsalted butter, softened
- 1/2 cup (100g) granulated sugar
- 2 large eggs
- 1 teaspoon vanilla extract
- 1 cup (125g) all-purpose flour
- 1 teaspoon baking powder

Instructions:

1. Prepare the Shortcrust Pastry:

- In a large mixing bowl, whisk together flour, sugar, baking powder, and salt.
- Add cold butter pieces and cut into the flour mixture using a pastry cutter or your fingers until it resembles coarse crumbs.
- Add the egg and mix until the dough comes together. It will be slightly crumbly but should hold together when pressed.
- Press the dough into the bottom of a greased 9x13-inch (23x33cm) baking dish, forming an even layer. Chill the dough-lined dish in the refrigerator while you prepare the other layers.

2. Prepare the Custard Layer:

- In a medium saucepan, heat milk over medium heat until it just begins to simmer.

- In a separate bowl, whisk together sugar, cornstarch, vanilla extract, and egg yolks until smooth and well combined.
- Gradually whisk the hot milk into the egg mixture, whisking constantly to prevent the eggs from curdling.
- Pour the mixture back into the saucepan and cook over medium heat, whisking constantly, until the custard thickens and comes to a boil (about 5-7 minutes).
- Remove from heat and let the custard cool slightly.

3. Prepare the Cake Layer:

- In a large mixing bowl, cream together softened butter and sugar until light and fluffy.
- Add eggs one at a time, beating well after each addition. Stir in vanilla extract.
- In a separate bowl, whisk together flour and baking powder. Gradually add the flour mixture to the butter mixture, mixing until just combined.

4. Assemble the Eierschecke:

- Preheat your oven to 350°F (175°C).
- Spread the cooled custard evenly over the chilled shortcrust pastry in the baking dish.
- Gently spread the cake batter over the custard layer, smoothing the top with a spatula.

5. Bake:

- Bake in the preheated oven for 30-35 minutes, or until the cake layer is golden brown and a toothpick inserted into the center comes out clean.

6. Cool and Serve:

- Let the Eierschecke cool completely in the baking dish on a wire rack.
- Once cooled, slice into squares or rectangles and serve at room temperature. Optionally, dust with powdered sugar before serving.

Enjoy this delightful and layered German dessert, Eierschecke, with its creamy custard and cake layers! It's perfect for sharing with friends and family over coffee or tea.

Stollen

Ingredients:

For the Stollen:

- 1 cup (150g) mixed dried fruits (such as raisins, currants, candied citrus peel)
- 1/2 cup (75g) chopped almonds or hazelnuts
- 1/4 cup (60ml) rum or orange juice
- 4 cups (500g) all-purpose flour
- 1/2 cup (100g) granulated sugar
- 2 teaspoons active dry yeast
- 1 teaspoon salt
- 1 teaspoon ground cinnamon
- 1/2 teaspoon ground nutmeg
- 1/2 teaspoon ground cardamom
- 1/2 cup (120ml) warm milk
- 1/2 cup (115g) unsalted butter, melted and cooled
- 2 large eggs, beaten
- Zest of 1 lemon
- Zest of 1 orange

For Assembly and Topping:

- 1/2 cup (115g) unsalted butter, melted
- Powdered sugar, for dusting

Instructions:

1. Prepare the Fruits and Nuts:

- In a small bowl, combine the mixed dried fruits and chopped nuts. Pour rum or orange juice over them and let soak for at least 1 hour, preferably overnight, to plump up the fruits.

2. Make the Dough:

- In a large mixing bowl, combine flour, sugar, yeast, salt, cinnamon, nutmeg, and cardamom.
- In a separate bowl, whisk together warm milk, melted butter, beaten eggs, lemon zest, and orange zest.
- Pour the wet ingredients into the dry ingredients and mix until a dough forms.
- Turn the dough out onto a lightly floured surface and knead for about 8-10 minutes, or until the dough is smooth and elastic.
- Drain the soaked fruits and nuts, discarding any excess liquid, and knead them into the dough until evenly distributed.

3. First Rise:

- Place the dough in a greased bowl, turning once to coat. Cover with a clean kitchen towel or plastic wrap and let rise in a warm place for 1-2 hours, or until doubled in size.

4. Shape the Stollen:

- Punch down the dough to deflate it and divide it into two equal portions.
- Roll each portion into an oval or rectangle shape, about 1 inch (2.5cm) thick.
- Fold one long side of the dough over to the other long side, leaving a slight overhang. Press the edge to seal and shape it into a slightly flattened oval loaf.
- Transfer the shaped loaves to parchment-lined baking sheets.

5. Second Rise:

- Cover the loaves loosely with a clean kitchen towel and let them rise in a warm place for another 30-45 minutes, or until slightly puffed.

6. Bake:

- Preheat your oven to 350°F (175°C).
- Bake the Stollen loaves in the preheated oven for 25-30 minutes, or until golden brown and the loaves sound hollow when tapped on the bottom.

7. Finish and Serve:

- While still warm, brush the tops of the Stollen with melted butter.
- Dust generously with powdered sugar while the loaves are still warm, and again once cooled.
- Let the Stollen cool completely on wire racks before slicing and serving.

8. Storage:

- Stollen can be stored in an airtight container at room temperature for up to 1 week, or frozen for longer storage. It actually improves in flavor after a few days as the flavors meld together.

Enjoy your homemade Stollen, a delicious and festive treat that's perfect for Christmas or any special occasion during the winter season!

Baumkuchen (Tree Cake)

Ingredients:

For the Batter:

- 1 cup (225g) unsalted butter, softened
- 1 cup (200g) granulated sugar
- 6 large eggs
- 1 teaspoon vanilla extract
- 1 cup (125g) all-purpose flour
- 1/2 cup (60g) cornstarch
- 1/4 teaspoon salt

For Assembly and Topping:

- 1/4 cup (50g) apricot jam or preserves
- 1/2 cup (60g) powdered sugar, for dusting

Equipment Needed:

- Round cake pan or springform pan (8-9 inches / 20-23cm diameter)
- Broiler or oven set to broil

Instructions:

1. Prepare the Batter:

- Preheat your broiler or set your oven to the highest broil setting. Place a rack in the upper third of the oven.
- In a large mixing bowl, cream together softened butter and sugar until light and fluffy.
- Add eggs one at a time, beating well after each addition. Stir in vanilla extract.
- In a separate bowl, sift together flour, cornstarch, and salt.
- Gradually add the flour mixture to the butter mixture, mixing until smooth and well combined. The batter should be thick but pourable.

2. Assembly and Baking:

- Grease the cake pan generously with butter or oil.
- Pour a thin layer of batter into the greased pan, spreading it evenly with a spatula. Place the pan under the broiler or in the oven and broil for 1-2 minutes, or until the top is golden brown and set.
- Remove the pan from the oven and carefully pour another thin layer of batter over the first layer, spreading it evenly. Broil again for 1-2 minutes until golden brown.
- Repeat this process of layering and broiling until all the batter is used up, ending with a final layer on top.

3. Final Touches:

- Once the Baumkuchen is fully baked and golden brown, remove it from the oven and let it cool slightly in the pan.
- While still warm, carefully remove the cake from the pan and transfer it to a wire rack to cool completely.
- Heat apricot jam or preserves in a small saucepan until melted and smooth. Brush the warm jam over the top and sides of the Baumkuchen to glaze.
- Dust generously with powdered sugar while the glaze is still warm.

4. Serve:

- Once cooled and glazed, slice the Baumkuchen into thin, even slices to showcase the layers and ring pattern.
- Serve at room temperature as a delightful dessert or treat with coffee or tea.

Tips:

- This simplified recipe uses the broiler method for baking layers quickly. Traditional Baumkuchen involves rotating the spit manually over a fire or heat source, creating the characteristic rings. For a more authentic approach, you can try using a spit or rotating skewer over a grill or broiler.
- Experiment with different jams or preserves for glazing, such as raspberry or apricot, to add extra flavor.

Enjoy making and savoring Baumkuchen, a delicious German treat that's as fun to bake as it is to eat!

Mohnkuchen (Poppy Seed Cake)

Ingredients:

For the Cake:

- 1 cup (200g) granulated sugar
- 1 cup (225g) unsalted butter, softened
- 4 large eggs
- 2 cups (250g) all-purpose flour
- 2 teaspoons baking powder
- 1/2 cup (120ml) milk
- 1 cup (120g) ground poppy seeds
- Zest of 1 lemon
- 1/4 cup (60ml) lemon juice

For the Topping:

- 1/2 cup (100g) granulated sugar
- 1/2 cup (120ml) heavy cream
- 1/2 cup (60g) sliced almonds (optional)

Instructions:

1. Prepare the Cake:

- Preheat your oven to 350°F (175°C). Grease and flour a 9x13-inch (23x33cm) baking dish or line it with parchment paper.
- In a large mixing bowl, cream together softened butter and sugar until light and fluffy.
- Add eggs one at a time, beating well after each addition.
- In a separate bowl, whisk together flour and baking powder. Gradually add the flour mixture to the butter mixture, alternating with milk, beginning and ending with the flour mixture. Mix until just combined.
- Stir in ground poppy seeds, lemon zest, and lemon juice until evenly distributed.
- Pour the batter into the prepared baking dish, spreading it evenly with a spatula.

2. Prepare the Topping:

- In a small bowl, mix together sugar and heavy cream until well combined.
- Pour the cream mixture evenly over the cake batter. If desired, sprinkle sliced almonds on top.

3. Bake:

- Bake in the preheated oven for 30-35 minutes, or until the cake is golden brown and a toothpick inserted into the center comes out clean.

4. Cool and Serve:

- Let the Mohnkuchen cool in the baking dish on a wire rack for about 15 minutes.
- Slice and serve the cake warm or at room temperature. Optionally, dust with powdered sugar before serving.

5. Storage:

- Store any leftover Mohnkuchen in an airtight container at room temperature for up to 3 days, or refrigerate for longer freshness.

Enjoy this delicious Mohnkuchen with its unique poppy seed flavor and moist texture, perfect for a special dessert or afternoon treat!

Quarkstollen (Quark-filled Stollen)

Ingredients:

For the Stollen Dough:

- 4 cups (500g) all-purpose flour
- 1/2 cup (100g) granulated sugar
- 1 teaspoon salt
- 1 tablespoon active dry yeast
- 3/4 cup (180ml) warm milk
- 1/2 cup (115g) unsalted butter, softened
- 1 cup (250g) quark cheese
- 1/2 cup (100g) raisins
- 1/2 cup (100g) dried cranberries or cherries
- Zest of 1 lemon
- Zest of 1 orange
- 1/2 cup (60g) slivered almonds

For Assembling and Baking:

- 1/2 cup (115g) unsalted butter, melted
- Powdered sugar, for dusting

Instructions:

1. Prepare the Dough:

- In a large mixing bowl, combine flour, sugar, and salt. Make a well in the center.
- Dissolve yeast in warm milk and pour into the well of the flour mixture. Let it sit for about 5-10 minutes, until frothy.
- Add softened butter and quark cheese to the flour mixture. Mix well until a dough forms.
- Knead the dough on a lightly floured surface for about 8-10 minutes, or until smooth and elastic.
- Mix in raisins, dried cranberries or cherries, lemon zest, orange zest, and slivered almonds until evenly distributed.
- Place the dough in a greased bowl, cover with a clean kitchen towel or plastic wrap, and let it rise in a warm place for about 1-2 hours, or until doubled in size.

2. Shape and Assemble:

- Preheat your oven to 350°F (175°C). Line a baking sheet with parchment paper.
- Punch down the risen dough and divide it into two equal portions.
- Roll each portion into an oval or rectangle shape, about 1 inch (2.5cm) thick.
- Fold one long side of the dough over to the other long side, leaving a slight overhang. Press the edge to seal and shape it into a slightly flattened oval loaf.

- Place the shaped loaves onto the prepared baking sheet.

3. Bake:

- Bake in the preheated oven for 30-35 minutes, or until golden brown and the loaves sound hollow when tapped on the bottom.

4. Finish:

- While still warm, brush the tops and sides of the Stollen loaves with melted butter.
- Dust generously with powdered sugar while the loaves are still warm.

5. Serve:

- Once cooled, slice the Quarkstollen into thin slices to reveal the filling and enjoy the rich, flavorful Stollen with a cup of coffee or tea.

6. Storage:

- Quarkstollen can be stored in an airtight container at room temperature for several days. It also freezes well for longer storage.

Enjoy making and sharing this delicious Quarkstollen, a wonderful twist on the classic German holiday treat!

Rote Grütze Torte (Red Berry Pudding Cake)

Ingredients:

For the Cake Base:

- 1 1/2 cups (190g) all-purpose flour
- 1 teaspoon baking powder
- 1/4 teaspoon salt
- 1/2 cup (115g) unsalted butter, softened
- 1 cup (200g) granulated sugar
- 2 large eggs
- 1 teaspoon vanilla extract
- 1/2 cup (120ml) milk

For the Rote Grütze Filling:

- 4 cups mixed red berries (such as strawberries, raspberries, red currants, cherries)
- 1/2 cup (100g) granulated sugar
- 1/4 cup (60ml) water
- Juice of 1 lemon
- 3 tablespoons cornstarch
- 1/4 cup (60ml) cold water

For Assembly:

- 1 cup (240ml) heavy cream, whipped (optional)
- Fresh berries for garnish (optional)

Instructions:

1. Prepare the Cake Base:

- Preheat your oven to 350°F (175°C). Grease and flour a 9-inch (23cm) springform pan or line it with parchment paper.
- In a medium bowl, whisk together flour, baking powder, and salt.
- In a large mixing bowl, cream together softened butter and sugar until light and fluffy.
- Add eggs one at a time, beating well after each addition. Stir in vanilla extract.
- Gradually add the flour mixture to the butter mixture, alternating with milk, beginning and ending with the flour mixture. Mix until just combined.
- Pour the batter into the prepared springform pan and spread it evenly with a spatula.
- Bake in the preheated oven for 25-30 minutes, or until a toothpick inserted into the center comes out clean.
- Remove from the oven and let the cake cool completely in the pan on a wire rack.

2. Prepare the Rote Grütze Filling:

- In a large saucepan, combine mixed red berries, sugar, water, and lemon juice. Bring to a simmer over medium heat.
- In a small bowl, whisk together cornstarch and cold water until smooth. Gradually stir the cornstarch mixture into the simmering berries.
- Cook, stirring constantly, until the mixture thickens to a pudding-like consistency, about 5-7 minutes.
- Remove from heat and let the Rote Grütze filling cool slightly.

3. Assemble the Rote Grütze Torte:

- Once the cake and Rote Grütze filling are cooled, carefully remove the cake from the springform pan and place it on a serving plate or cake stand.
- Spread the cooled Rote Grütze filling evenly over the top of the cake.
- Optionally, spread whipped cream over the Rote Grütze filling for an extra creamy layer.
- Garnish with fresh berries on top, if desired.

4. Chill and Serve:

- Refrigerate the Rote Grütze Torte for at least 1 hour before serving to allow the flavors to meld together.
- Slice and serve chilled. Enjoy the refreshing and fruity flavors of this traditional German dessert!

Rote Grütze Torte is perfect for summer gatherings or any time you want to enjoy the bright flavors of red berries in a delightful cake form. It's sure to be a hit with family and friends!

Käsekuchen (German Cheesecake)

Ingredients:

For the Crust:

- 1 1/2 cups (180g) all-purpose flour
- 1/2 cup (100g) granulated sugar
- 1/2 cup (115g) unsalted butter, cold and cut into small pieces
- 1 large egg

For the Filling:

- 1 lb (450g) quark cheese (or substitute with cream cheese or ricotta cheese)
- 1 cup (200g) granulated sugar
- 4 large eggs, separated
- Zest and juice of 1 lemon
- 1 teaspoon vanilla extract
- 1/2 cup (120ml) heavy cream
- 1/4 cup (30g) all-purpose flour
- Powdered sugar, for dusting

Instructions:

1. Prepare the Crust:

- Preheat your oven to 350°F (175°C). Grease a 9-inch (23cm) springform pan or line it with parchment paper.
- In a large mixing bowl, combine flour and sugar. Add cold butter pieces and cut into the flour mixture using a pastry cutter or your fingers until it resembles coarse crumbs.
- Add the egg and mix until the dough comes together. Press the dough evenly into the bottom of the prepared springform pan.
- Bake the crust in the preheated oven for 15 minutes, or until lightly golden. Remove from the oven and let it cool while preparing the filling.

2. Prepare the Filling:

- In a large mixing bowl, beat quark cheese (or substitute) and granulated sugar until smooth and creamy.
- Add egg yolks, lemon zest, lemon juice, and vanilla extract to the cheese mixture. Mix well until fully combined.
- In a separate bowl, whip the egg whites until stiff peaks form.
- Gently fold the whipped egg whites into the cheese mixture.
- In another bowl, whip the heavy cream until stiff peaks form. Fold the whipped cream into the cheese mixture as well.
- Finally, fold in the flour until just combined.

3. Assemble and Bake:

- Pour the filling over the cooled crust in the springform pan, spreading it evenly with a spatula.
- Bake in the preheated oven for 50-60 minutes, or until the cheesecake is set and the top is lightly golden brown. The center may still jiggle slightly, but it will set as it cools.

4. Cool and Serve:

- Remove the Käsekuchen from the oven and let it cool completely in the pan on a wire rack.
- Once cooled, refrigerate the cheesecake for at least 2 hours (preferably overnight) to allow it to firm up.
- Before serving, dust the top with powdered sugar.

5. Serve:

- Slice and serve chilled, optionally with fresh berries or a fruit compote on the side.

Enjoy the creamy and delightful flavors of German Käsekuchen, a perfect dessert for any occasion or as a treat with coffee or tea!

Nusstorte (Nut Cake)

Ingredients:

For the Cake Layers:

- 1 cup (100g) ground walnuts
- 1 cup (100g) ground hazelnuts
- 1 cup (125g) all-purpose flour
- 1 teaspoon baking powder
- 1/2 teaspoon ground cinnamon
- 1/4 teaspoon salt
- 4 large eggs, separated
- 1 cup (200g) granulated sugar
- Zest of 1 lemon
- Zest of 1 orange

For the Filling:

- 1 cup (250ml) heavy cream
- 1/2 cup (100g) granulated sugar
- 1 teaspoon vanilla extract
- 1 cup (100g) ground walnuts
- 1 cup (100g) ground hazelnuts

For Assembly and Decoration:

- 1/2 cup (120ml) rum or water (for moistening)
- Powdered sugar, for dusting

Instructions:

1. Prepare the Cake Layers:

- Preheat your oven to 350°F (175°C). Grease and flour two 9-inch (23cm) round cake pans or line them with parchment paper.
- In a medium bowl, combine ground walnuts, ground hazelnuts, flour, baking powder, ground cinnamon, and salt. Mix well and set aside.
- In a large mixing bowl, beat egg yolks and granulated sugar until pale and creamy. Stir in lemon zest and orange zest.
- Gradually fold the nut-flour mixture into the egg yolk mixture until well combined.
- In another bowl, beat egg whites until stiff peaks form. Gently fold the beaten egg whites into the batter until just incorporated.
- Divide the batter evenly between the prepared cake pans, spreading it into an even layer with a spatula.

- Bake in the preheated oven for 20-25 minutes, or until a toothpick inserted into the center comes out clean.
- Remove from the oven and let the cake layers cool in the pans for 10 minutes before transferring them to a wire rack to cool completely.

2. Prepare the Filling:

- In a medium bowl, whip heavy cream, granulated sugar, and vanilla extract until stiff peaks form.
- Gently fold in ground walnuts and ground hazelnuts until evenly distributed.

3. Assemble the Nusstorte:

- Place one cake layer on a serving plate or cake stand. Moisten the top of the cake layer with rum or water using a pastry brush.
- Spread half of the nut filling evenly over the moistened cake layer.
- Place the second cake layer on top of the filling. Moisten the top of this layer with rum or water as well.
- Spread the remaining nut filling evenly over the top of the second cake layer.

4. Decoration:

- Dust the top of the Nusstorte generously with powdered sugar.
- Optionally, decorate with whole or chopped nuts on top for added texture and presentation.

5. Serve:

- Chill the Nusstorte in the refrigerator for at least 2 hours before serving to allow the flavors to meld together and the filling to set.
- Slice and serve chilled, optionally with whipped cream or a scoop of vanilla ice cream.

Enjoy this rich and nutty Nusstorte as a delightful dessert for special occasions or as a treat with coffee or tea!

Erdbeerkuchen (Strawberry Cake)

Ingredients:

For the Cake Base:

- 1 1/2 cups (190g) all-purpose flour
- 1 1/2 teaspoons baking powder
- 1/4 teaspoon salt
- 1/2 cup (115g) unsalted butter, softened
- 3/4 cup (150g) granulated sugar
- 2 large eggs
- 1 teaspoon vanilla extract
- 1/2 cup (120ml) milk

For the Strawberry Topping:

- 1 lb (450g) fresh strawberries, hulled and sliced
- 1/4 cup (50g) granulated sugar
- 1 tablespoon cornstarch
- Juice of 1/2 lemon

For Assembly and Decoration:

- Powdered sugar, for dusting
- Fresh mint leaves, for garnish (optional)
- Whipped cream or vanilla ice cream (optional, for serving)

Instructions:

1. Prepare the Cake Base:

- Preheat your oven to 350°F (175°C). Grease and flour a 9-inch (23cm) round cake pan or line it with parchment paper.
- In a medium bowl, whisk together flour, baking powder, and salt.
- In a large mixing bowl, cream together softened butter and granulated sugar until light and fluffy.
- Add eggs one at a time, beating well after each addition. Stir in vanilla extract.
- Gradually add the flour mixture to the butter mixture, alternating with milk, beginning and ending with the flour mixture. Mix until just combined.
- Pour the batter into the prepared cake pan, spreading it evenly with a spatula.
- Bake in the preheated oven for 25-30 minutes, or until a toothpick inserted into the center comes out clean.
- Remove from the oven and let the cake cool in the pan for 10 minutes before transferring it to a wire rack to cool completely.

2. Prepare the Strawberry Topping:

- In a medium saucepan, combine sliced strawberries, granulated sugar, cornstarch, and lemon juice.
- Cook over medium heat, stirring constantly, until the mixture thickens and the strawberries release their juices, about 5-7 minutes.
- Remove from heat and let the strawberry topping cool slightly.

3. Assemble the Erdbeerkuchen:

- Once the cake base is completely cooled, carefully transfer it to a serving platter or cake stand.
- Spoon the strawberry topping evenly over the top of the cake, spreading it gently with a spatula.

4. Decoration and Serving:

- Dust the top of the Erdbeerkuchen with powdered sugar.
- Optionally, garnish with fresh mint leaves for added freshness and presentation.
- Serve slices of Erdbeerkuchen plain or with a dollop of whipped cream or a scoop of vanilla ice cream, if desired.

Enjoy this delicious and fruity Erdbeerkuchen, perfect for celebrating the sweetness of fresh strawberries in a delightful cake form!

Russischer Zupfkuchen (Russian Cheesecake Brownie)

Ingredients:

For the Chocolate Dough:

- 2 cups (250g) all-purpose flour
- 3/4 cup (150g) granulated sugar
- 1/2 teaspoon baking powder
- 1/4 teaspoon salt
- 3/4 cup (170g) unsalted butter, softened
- 1/4 cup (25g) unsweetened cocoa powder
- 1 large egg

For the Cheesecake Filling:

- 1 lb (450g) quark cheese (or substitute with cream cheese or ricotta cheese)
- 3/4 cup (150g) granulated sugar
- 2 large eggs
- 1 teaspoon vanilla extract
- 1/4 cup (60g) unsalted butter, melted
- 1/4 cup (30g) all-purpose flour

For Assembly:

- Powdered sugar, for dusting

Instructions:

1. Prepare the Chocolate Dough:

- In a large mixing bowl, combine flour, sugar, baking powder, and salt.
- Add softened butter, cocoa powder, and egg to the flour mixture. Mix until a dough forms. You can use your hands to knead the dough together until smooth.
- Divide the dough into two portions: one larger portion for the base and a smaller portion for the topping. Wrap each portion separately in plastic wrap and chill in the refrigerator for at least 30 minutes.

2. Prepare the Cheesecake Filling:

- In a large mixing bowl, beat quark cheese (or substitute) and granulated sugar until smooth.
- Add eggs, one at a time, beating well after each addition.
- Stir in vanilla extract, melted butter, and flour until well combined. Set aside.

3. Assemble the Russischer Zupfkuchen:

- Preheat your oven to 350°F (175°C). Grease a 9-inch (23cm) springform pan or line it with parchment paper.
- Take the larger portion of chilled chocolate dough and press it evenly into the bottom and slightly up the sides of the prepared springform pan to form the base.
- Pour the prepared cheesecake filling over the chocolate dough base, spreading it evenly with a spatula.
- Take the smaller portion of chilled chocolate dough and crumble it evenly over the top of the cheesecake filling.

4. Bake:

- Bake in the preheated oven for 50-60 minutes, or until the top is set and the edges are lightly golden brown. The center may still jiggle slightly, but it will set as it cools.

5. Cool and Serve:

- Remove the Russischer Zupfkuchen from the oven and let it cool completely in the pan on a wire rack.
- Once cooled, carefully remove the sides of the springform pan.
- Dust the top of the Russischer Zupfkuchen with powdered sugar before slicing and serving.

Enjoy this delightful combination of chocolate and creamy cheesecake in every bite of Russischer Zupfkuchen! It's perfect for any occasion or as a treat with coffee or tea.

Mohrenkopftorte (Chocolate Marshmallow Cake)

Ingredients:

For the Chocolate Cake:

- 1 1/2 cups (190g) all-purpose flour
- 1 cup (200g) granulated sugar
- 1/2 cup (50g) unsweetened cocoa powder
- 1 1/2 teaspoons baking powder
- 1 teaspoon baking soda
- 1/2 teaspoon salt
- 2 large eggs
- 1 cup (240ml) buttermilk
- 1/2 cup (120ml) vegetable oil
- 2 teaspoons vanilla extract
- 1 cup (240ml) boiling water

For the Marshmallow Topping:

- 3/4 cup (150g) granulated sugar
- 1/2 cup (120ml) water
- 2 large egg whites
- 1/4 teaspoon cream of tartar
- 1 teaspoon vanilla extract

For Assembly and Decoration:

- 1 cup (240ml) heavy cream, whipped
- Chocolate shavings or sprinkles (optional)
- Fresh berries for garnish (optional)

Instructions:

1. Prepare the Chocolate Cake:

- Preheat your oven to 350°F (175°C). Grease and flour two 9-inch (23cm) round cake pans or line them with parchment paper.
- In a large mixing bowl, sift together flour, sugar, cocoa powder, baking powder, baking soda, and salt.
- Add eggs, buttermilk, vegetable oil, and vanilla extract to the flour mixture. Beat on medium speed for 2 minutes.
- Stir in boiling water until the batter is well combined and smooth. The batter will be thin.
- Pour the batter evenly into the prepared cake pans.
- Bake in the preheated oven for 30-35 minutes, or until a toothpick inserted into the center comes out clean.

- Remove from the oven and let the cakes cool in the pans for 10 minutes before transferring them to a wire rack to cool completely.

2. Prepare the Marshmallow Topping:

- In a medium saucepan, combine sugar and water. Heat over medium-high heat, stirring constantly, until the sugar dissolves and the mixture comes to a boil.
- Continue boiling without stirring until the mixture reaches 240°F (115°C) on a candy thermometer, or until it forms a soft ball when a small amount is dropped into cold water.
- While the sugar syrup is heating, in a large mixing bowl, beat egg whites and cream of tartar until soft peaks form.
- Gradually pour the hot sugar syrup into the egg whites, beating continuously on high speed until stiff peaks form and the mixture is thick and glossy. This is your marshmallow topping.
- Beat in vanilla extract until well combined.

3. Assemble the Mohrenkopftorte:

- Place one chocolate cake layer on a serving plate or cake stand.
- Spread a layer of whipped cream evenly over the top of the cake layer.
- Carefully spread half of the marshmallow topping over the whipped cream layer, spreading it evenly with a spatula.
- Place the second chocolate cake layer on top of the marshmallow topping.
- Spread another layer of whipped cream over the top of the second cake layer.
- Spread the remaining marshmallow topping evenly over the whipped cream layer.

4. Decoration:

- Optionally, decorate the Mohrenkopftorte with chocolate shavings or sprinkles on top.
- Garnish with fresh berries around the edge of the cake, if desired.

5. Chill and Serve:

- Refrigerate the Mohrenkopftorte for at least 2 hours before serving to allow the flavors to meld together and the marshmallow topping to set.
- Slice and serve chilled. Enjoy the decadent combination of chocolate cake and fluffy marshmallow topping in each delicious bite!

Mohrenkopftorte is a delightful treat that's sure to impress with its rich flavors and creamy texture. It's perfect for special occasions or as a delightful dessert after a meal.

Apfelstrudel (Apple Strudel)

Ingredients:

For the Strudel Dough:

- 2 cups (250g) all-purpose flour
- 1/4 teaspoon salt
- 1 large egg
- 1/2 cup (120ml) lukewarm water
- 2 tablespoons vegetable oil
- 1 tablespoon white vinegar

For the Apple Filling:

- 6-7 medium apples (such as Granny Smith or Braeburn), peeled, cored, and thinly sliced
- 1/2 cup (100g) granulated sugar
- 1 cup (100g) breadcrumbs
- 1/2 cup (115g) unsalted butter, melted
- 1 teaspoon ground cinnamon
- 1/2 cup (50g) raisins (optional)
- Zest of 1 lemon
- Juice of 1/2 lemon

For Assembly:

- Powdered sugar, for dusting
- Vanilla ice cream or whipped cream, for serving (optional)

Instructions:

1. Prepare the Strudel Dough:

- In a large mixing bowl, sift together flour and salt.
- In a separate bowl, whisk together egg, lukewarm water, vegetable oil, and white vinegar.
- Make a well in the center of the flour mixture and pour in the wet ingredients. Stir with a wooden spoon until the dough comes together.
- Knead the dough on a lightly floured surface for about 10 minutes, until smooth and elastic. Shape into a ball and coat lightly with oil. Cover with a damp cloth and let rest at room temperature for 30 minutes.

2. Prepare the Apple Filling:

- In a large bowl, toss together sliced apples, granulated sugar, ground cinnamon, lemon zest, and lemon juice until well combined. If using raisins, mix them in as well.

- In a small pan, melt the butter over low heat. Add breadcrumbs and toast them until golden brown, stirring constantly to prevent burning. Remove from heat and let cool.

3. Assemble the Apfelstrudel:

- Preheat your oven to 350°F (175°C). Line a baking sheet with parchment paper.
- On a clean, lightly floured kitchen towel, roll out the rested dough into a thin rectangle, gently stretching it with your hands until it is almost transparent.
- Brush the entire surface of the dough with melted butter, leaving a small border around the edges.
- Evenly sprinkle the toasted breadcrumbs over the buttered dough, creating a layer to absorb excess moisture from the apples.
- Spread the apple filling evenly over the breadcrumbs.
- Fold in the short sides of the dough over the filling, then use the towel to lift and roll the dough, jelly-roll style, starting from the long edge closest to you. Tuck in the ends to seal.
- Carefully transfer the rolled strudel onto the prepared baking sheet, seam side down.

4. Bake the Apfelstrudel:

- Brush the top of the strudel with any remaining melted butter.
- Bake in the preheated oven for 45-50 minutes, or until the strudel is golden brown and crispy.

5. Serve:

- Remove the Apfelstrudel from the oven and let it cool slightly on the baking sheet.
- Dust generously with powdered sugar before slicing.
- Serve warm slices of Apfelstrudel with a scoop of vanilla ice cream or a dollop of whipped cream, if desired.

Enjoy the delightful flavors of Apfelstrudel, a perfect dessert that's warm, comforting, and filled with the goodness of spiced apples wrapped in crisp, flaky pastry!

Himbeertorte (Raspberry Cake)

Ingredients:

For the Cake:

- 1 1/2 cups (190g) all-purpose flour
- 1 1/2 teaspoons baking powder
- 1/2 teaspoon baking soda
- 1/4 teaspoon salt
- 1/2 cup (115g) unsalted butter, softened
- 1 cup (200g) granulated sugar
- 2 large eggs
- 1 teaspoon vanilla extract
- 1 cup (240ml) buttermilk

For the Raspberry Filling:

- 3 cups (about 360g) fresh raspberries, divided
- 1/4 cup (50g) granulated sugar
- 2 tablespoons cornstarch
- Juice of 1/2 lemon

For the Whipped Cream Frosting:

- 2 cups (480ml) heavy cream, chilled
- 1/2 cup (60g) powdered sugar
- 1 teaspoon vanilla extract

For Assembly and Decoration:

- Additional fresh raspberries, for garnish
- Mint leaves, for garnish (optional)
- Powdered sugar, for dusting (optional)

Instructions:

1. Prepare the Cake:

- Preheat your oven to 350°F (175°C). Grease and flour two 9-inch (23cm) round cake pans or line them with parchment paper.
- In a medium bowl, whisk together flour, baking powder, baking soda, and salt.
- In a large mixing bowl, cream together softened butter and granulated sugar until light and fluffy.
- Add eggs one at a time, beating well after each addition. Stir in vanilla extract.

- Gradually add the flour mixture to the butter mixture, alternating with buttermilk, beginning and ending with the flour mixture. Mix until just combined.
- Divide the batter evenly between the prepared cake pans, spreading it into an even layer with a spatula.
- Bake in the preheated oven for 20-25 minutes, or until a toothpick inserted into the center comes out clean.
- Remove from the oven and let the cakes cool in the pans for 10 minutes before transferring them to a wire rack to cool completely.

2. Prepare the Raspberry Filling:

- In a saucepan, combine 2 cups of raspberries (reserve 1 cup for decoration), granulated sugar, cornstarch, and lemon juice.
- Cook over medium heat, stirring frequently, until the raspberries break down and the mixture thickens, about 5-7 minutes.
- Remove from heat and strain through a fine mesh sieve to remove seeds, if desired. Let the raspberry filling cool completely.

3. Prepare the Whipped Cream Frosting:

- In a large mixing bowl, beat chilled heavy cream, powdered sugar, and vanilla extract until stiff peaks form.

4. Assemble the Himbeertorte:

- Place one cooled cake layer on a serving plate or cake stand.
- Spread a layer of whipped cream frosting evenly over the top of the cake layer.
- Spoon the cooled raspberry filling over the whipped cream frosting, spreading it evenly.
- Place the second cake layer on top of the raspberry filling.

5. Frost and Decorate:

- Frost the top and sides of the cake with the remaining whipped cream frosting.
- Garnish with fresh raspberries and mint leaves, if desired.
- Dust the top of the cake with powdered sugar for an elegant finish.

6. Chill and Serve:

- Refrigerate the Himbeertorte for at least 1 hour before serving to allow the flavors to meld together.
- Slice and serve chilled. Enjoy the refreshing and fruity flavors of this delicious Himbeertorte!

This Himbeertorte is perfect for special occasions or as a delightful treat with afternoon tea. The combination of moist cake, tart raspberry filling, and light whipped cream frosting makes it a favorite among raspberry lovers!

Pflaumenmus Kuchen (Plum Butter Cake)

Ingredients:

For the Cake Base:

- 1 1/2 cups (190g) all-purpose flour
- 1 1/2 teaspoons baking powder
- 1/4 teaspoon salt
- 1/2 cup (115g) unsalted butter, softened
- 3/4 cup (150g) granulated sugar
- 2 large eggs
- 1 teaspoon vanilla extract
- 1/2 cup (120ml) milk

For the Plum Butter Topping:

- 1 1/2 cups (360g) Pflaumenmus (Plum Butter)
- 1/2 teaspoon ground cinnamon
- 1/4 teaspoon ground cloves

For Assembly:

- Powdered sugar, for dusting

Instructions:

1. Prepare the Cake Base:

- Preheat your oven to 350°F (175°C). Grease and flour a 9x13-inch (23x33cm) baking pan or line it with parchment paper.
- In a medium bowl, whisk together flour, baking powder, and salt.
- In a large mixing bowl, cream together softened butter and granulated sugar until light and fluffy.
- Add eggs one at a time, beating well after each addition. Stir in vanilla extract.
- Gradually add the flour mixture to the butter mixture, alternating with milk, beginning and ending with the flour mixture. Mix until just combined.
- Spread the cake batter evenly into the prepared baking pan, using a spatula to smooth the top.

2. Prepare the Plum Butter Topping:

- In a small bowl, mix together Pflaumenmus (Plum Butter), ground cinnamon, and ground cloves until well combined.
- Spoon the plum butter mixture evenly over the top of the cake batter in the baking pan, spreading it gently with a spatula to cover the entire surface.

3. Bake:

- Bake in the preheated oven for 30-35 minutes, or until the cake is golden brown and a toothpick inserted into the center comes out clean.

4. Cool and Serve:

- Remove the cake from the oven and let it cool completely in the pan on a wire rack.
- Once cooled, dust the top of the Pflaumenmus Kuchen with powdered sugar.
- Slice into squares and serve at room temperature or slightly warmed, as desired.

Enjoy the comforting flavors of this Pflaumenmus Kuchen, perfect for serving as a delicious dessert or with coffee or tea for a delightful afternoon treat!

Prinzregententorte

Ingredients:

For the Sponge Cake Layers:

- 8 large eggs, separated
- 1 cup (200g) granulated sugar
- 1 cup (120g) all-purpose flour
- 1/2 cup (60g) cornstarch
- 1 teaspoon baking powder

For the Chocolate Buttercream:

- 1 cup (225g) unsalted butter, softened
- 2 cups (240g) powdered sugar
- 4 ounces (120g) dark chocolate, melted and cooled
- 1 teaspoon vanilla extract

For the Chocolate Glaze:

- 4 ounces (120g) dark chocolate, chopped
- 1/2 cup (120ml) heavy cream

For Assembly and Decoration:

- 1/2 cup (50g) sliced almonds, toasted (optional)
- Cocoa powder, for dusting (optional)

Instructions:

1. Prepare the Sponge Cake Layers:

- Preheat your oven to 350°F (175°C). Grease and flour four 9-inch (23cm) round cake pans or line them with parchment paper.
- In a large mixing bowl, beat egg yolks and granulated sugar until pale and creamy.
- In another bowl, sift together flour, cornstarch, and baking powder.
- Gradually add the flour mixture to the egg yolk mixture, mixing until smooth.
- In a separate bowl, beat egg whites until stiff peaks form.
- Gently fold the beaten egg whites into the batter until well combined.
- Divide the batter evenly among the prepared cake pans, spreading it into an even layer.
- Bake in the preheated oven for 12-15 minutes, or until a toothpick inserted into the center of the cakes comes out clean.
- Remove from the oven and let the cakes cool in the pans for 10 minutes before transferring them to a wire rack to cool completely.

2. Prepare the Chocolate Buttercream:

- In a large mixing bowl, beat softened butter until creamy.
- Gradually add powdered sugar and beat until light and fluffy.
- Stir in melted and cooled dark chocolate and vanilla extract until smooth and well combined.

3. Assemble the Prinzregententorte:

- Place one sponge cake layer on a serving plate or cake stand.
- Spread a layer of chocolate buttercream evenly over the top of the cake layer.
- Repeat with the remaining cake layers and buttercream, stacking them on top of each other.
- Ensure the top layer is a sponge cake layer (without buttercream on top).

4. Prepare the Chocolate Glaze:

- In a small saucepan, heat heavy cream until just simmering (do not boil).
- Remove from heat and add chopped dark chocolate.
- Let it sit for 1-2 minutes, then stir until smooth and glossy.

5. Frost and Decorate:

- Pour the chocolate glaze over the top of the assembled cake, allowing it to drip down the sides.
- Optionally, sprinkle toasted sliced almonds over the top of the cake for decoration.
- Refrigerate the cake for at least 1 hour to set the glaze and firm up the layers.

6. Serve:

- Before serving, dust the top of the Prinzregententorte with cocoa powder, if desired.
- Slice and serve chilled. Enjoy the luxurious layers of chocolate and sponge in this elegant Prinzregententorte!

This cake is a labor of love but well worth the effort for special occasions, impressing guests, or simply treating yourself to a slice of Bavarian culinary history.

Windbeutel (Cream Puff Cake)

Ingredients:

For the Choux Pastry:

- 1 cup (240ml) water
- 1/2 cup (115g) unsalted butter
- 1/4 teaspoon salt
- 1 cup (125g) all-purpose flour
- 4 large eggs

For the Filling:

- 2 cups (480ml) heavy cream
- 1/4 cup (30g) powdered sugar
- 1 teaspoon vanilla extract
- Fresh berries or fruit for garnish (optional)
- Powdered sugar, for dusting

Instructions:

1. Prepare the Choux Pastry:

- Preheat your oven to 400°F (200°C). Line a baking sheet with parchment paper.
- In a medium saucepan, combine water, butter, and salt. Bring to a boil over medium-high heat.
- Reduce heat to low and add flour all at once. Stir vigorously with a wooden spoon until the mixture forms a ball and pulls away from the sides of the pan.
- Remove from heat and let cool for 5 minutes.
- Add eggs, one at a time, beating well after each addition, until the dough is smooth and glossy.
- Transfer the choux pastry dough to a piping bag fitted with a large round tip (or use a spoon).
- Pipe mounds of dough onto the prepared baking sheet, leaving space between each for expansion. Each mound should be about 2 inches (5 cm) in diameter.
- Bake in the preheated oven for 25-30 minutes, or until the puffs are golden brown and puffed up.
- Remove from the oven and transfer the puffs to a wire rack to cool completely.

2. Prepare the Filling:

- In a large mixing bowl, beat heavy cream, powdered sugar, and vanilla extract until stiff peaks form.
- Transfer the whipped cream into a piping bag fitted with a small round tip (or use a spoon).

3. Assemble the Windbeutel:

- Using a sharp knife, carefully slice each cooled puff horizontally, without cutting all the way through.
- Pipe or spoon whipped cream generously into each puff.
- Optional: Add fresh berries or fruit on top of the whipped cream.
- Place the top halves of the puffs gently over the whipped cream filling.

4. Serve:

- Arrange the filled Windbeutel on a serving platter.
- Dust with powdered sugar for a decorative finish.
- Serve immediately, or refrigerate until ready to serve.

Enjoy the light and airy texture of the choux pastry combined with the creamy filling in this delicious Windbeutel dessert! It's perfect for any occasion and sure to impress your guests with its classic German charm.

Schnecken (Cinnamon Rolls)

Ingredients:

For the Dough:

- 4 cups (500g) all-purpose flour
- 1/2 cup (100g) granulated sugar
- 2 teaspoons active dry yeast
- 1 teaspoon salt
- 1 cup (240ml) milk, lukewarm
- 1/2 cup (115g) unsalted butter, melted and cooled
- 2 large eggs

For the Filling:

- 1 cup (200g) brown sugar, packed
- 1/2 cup (115g) unsalted butter, softened
- 2 tablespoons ground cinnamon
- 1 cup (120g) chopped nuts or raisins (optional)

For the Glaze:

- 1 cup (120g) powdered sugar
- 2-3 tablespoons milk or cream
- 1/2 teaspoon vanilla extract

Instructions:

1. Prepare the Dough:

- In a large mixing bowl or the bowl of a stand mixer fitted with a dough hook, combine flour, granulated sugar, yeast, and salt.
- In a separate bowl, whisk together lukewarm milk, melted butter, and eggs.
- Gradually add the wet ingredients to the dry ingredients, mixing until a dough forms.
- Knead the dough for about 8-10 minutes until smooth and elastic. If using a stand mixer, knead on medium speed.
- Place the dough in a greased bowl, cover with a clean kitchen towel or plastic wrap, and let it rise in a warm place for about 1 hour or until doubled in size.

2. Prepare the Filling:

- In a medium bowl, mix together brown sugar, softened butter, and ground cinnamon until well combined.

3. Assemble the Schnecken:

- Punch down the risen dough and roll it out on a floured surface into a large rectangle, about 16x12 inches (40x30 cm).
- Spread the cinnamon filling evenly over the dough, leaving a small border around the edges. Sprinkle with chopped nuts or raisins, if using.
- Starting from the long edge, roll up the dough tightly into a log.
- Cut the log into 12 equal slices using a sharp knife or dental floss.
- Place the slices, cut side up, in a greased 9x13-inch (23x33 cm) baking pan or two 9-inch (23 cm) round cake pans.
- Cover the pan(s) with a clean kitchen towel and let the rolls rise again for about 30-45 minutes, until puffed up.

4. Bake the Schnecken:

- Preheat your oven to 350°F (175°C).
- Bake the rolls in the preheated oven for 25-30 minutes, or until golden brown and cooked through.
- Remove from the oven and let cool slightly in the pan on a wire rack.

5. Prepare the Glaze:

- In a small bowl, whisk together powdered sugar, milk or cream, and vanilla extract until smooth.

6. Glaze and Serve:

- Drizzle the glaze over the warm Schnecken rolls.
- Serve the rolls warm. Enjoy the wonderful aroma and flavors of these homemade Schnecken with a cup of coffee or tea!

These Schnecken are perfect for breakfast or as a sweet treat any time of day. They're sure to be a hit with family and friends!

Dampfnudeln (Steamed Dumplings)

Ingredients:

For the Dough:

- 4 cups (500g) all-purpose flour
- 1/4 cup (50g) granulated sugar
- 1 teaspoon salt
- 2 teaspoons active dry yeast
- 1 cup (240ml) lukewarm milk
- 1/4 cup (60g) unsalted butter, melted
- 2 large eggs

For Cooking:

- 1/4 cup (60g) unsalted butter
- 1/4 cup (50g) granulated sugar
- 1 cup (240ml) water

Instructions:

1. Prepare the Dough:

- In a large mixing bowl or the bowl of a stand mixer fitted with a dough hook, combine flour, sugar, salt, and yeast.
- In a separate bowl, whisk together lukewarm milk, melted butter, and eggs.
- Gradually add the wet ingredients to the dry ingredients, mixing until a dough forms.
- Knead the dough for about 8-10 minutes until smooth and elastic. If using a stand mixer, knead on medium speed.
- Place the dough in a greased bowl, cover with a clean kitchen towel or plastic wrap, and let it rise in a warm place for about 1 hour or until doubled in size.

2. Shape the Dampfnudeln:

- Punch down the risen dough and divide it into 12 equal portions. Shape each portion into a smooth ball.

3. Cook the Dampfnudeln:

- In a large, deep skillet or Dutch oven with a tight-fitting lid, melt butter over medium heat.
- Sprinkle sugar evenly over the melted butter and let it caramelize slightly.
- Place the dough balls into the skillet, spaced apart. Pour water around the edges of the skillet, not directly over the dough.

- Cover the skillet with the lid and reduce heat to low. Let the Dampfnudeln steam for about 20-25 minutes, or until they have doubled in size and the bottoms are golden brown and caramelized.

4. Serve:

- Remove the Dampfnudeln from the skillet and serve warm.
- They can be served with vanilla sauce, fruit compote, or enjoyed plain with a dusting of powdered sugar.

Enjoy these fluffy and delicious Dampfnudeln as a delightful German treat!

Berliner Pfannkuchen (Berlin Pancakes)

Ingredients:

For the Dough:

- 2 1/4 teaspoons (1 packet) active dry yeast
- 1/4 cup (60ml) lukewarm water
- 3 1/2 cups (440g) all-purpose flour
- 1/2 cup (100g) granulated sugar
- 1/2 teaspoon salt
- 1/2 cup (120ml) milk, lukewarm
- 3 large eggs
- 1/4 cup (60g) unsalted butter, softened

For Frying:

- Vegetable oil, for frying

For Filling and Decoration:

- Jam (apricot, raspberry, or strawberry)
- Powdered sugar, for dusting

Instructions:

1. Prepare the Dough:

- In a small bowl, dissolve the yeast in lukewarm water. Let it sit for about 5-10 minutes until foamy.
- In a large mixing bowl or the bowl of a stand mixer fitted with a dough hook, combine flour, sugar, and salt.
- Add the yeast mixture, lukewarm milk, eggs, and softened butter to the dry ingredients. Mix until a smooth dough forms.
- Knead the dough for about 5-7 minutes until it is smooth and elastic.
- Place the dough in a greased bowl, cover with a clean kitchen towel or plastic wrap, and let it rise in a warm place for about 1 hour or until doubled in size.

2. Shape and Fry the Berliner:

- Punch down the risen dough and divide it into 12 equal portions. Shape each portion into a smooth ball and place them on a baking sheet lined with parchment paper. Cover with a kitchen towel and let them rest for 15-20 minutes.
- In a large, deep skillet or Dutch oven, heat vegetable oil to 350°F (175°C) over medium heat.

- Carefully place the dough balls into the hot oil, a few at a time, without overcrowding the pan. Fry for about 3-4 minutes per side, or until golden brown and cooked through.
- Remove the Berliner from the oil using a slotted spoon and drain on paper towels. Let them cool slightly.

3. Fill the Berliner:

- Once cooled enough to handle, use a piping bag fitted with a long, narrow tip (or a squeeze bottle) to inject each Berliner with jam through a small slit on the side. Fill generously with your preferred jam.

4. Serve:

- Dust the filled Berliner Pfannkuchen with powdered sugar.
- Serve warm or at room temperature. Enjoy these delicious German pastries with a cup of coffee or tea!

These Berliner Pfannkuchen are perfect for breakfast, brunch, or as a sweet treat any time of day. They are best enjoyed fresh, so try to consume them soon after filling and dusting with powdered sugar for the best flavor and texture.

Streuselplätzchen (Streusel Cookies)

Ingredients:

For the Cookie Dough:

- 1 cup (225g) unsalted butter, softened
- 3/4 cup (150g) granulated sugar
- 1 teaspoon vanilla extract
- 2 large egg yolks
- 2 cups (250g) all-purpose flour
- 1/2 teaspoon baking powder
- 1/4 teaspoon salt

For the Streusel Topping:

- 1 cup (125g) all-purpose flour
- 1/2 cup (100g) granulated sugar
- 1/2 cup (115g) unsalted butter, melted
- 1 teaspoon ground cinnamon (optional)

Instructions:

1. Prepare the Cookie Dough:

- In a large mixing bowl, cream together softened butter and granulated sugar until light and fluffy.
- Add vanilla extract and egg yolks, mixing well after each addition.
- In a separate bowl, whisk together flour, baking powder, and salt.
- Gradually add the flour mixture to the butter mixture, mixing until a soft dough forms.
- Cover the cookie dough with plastic wrap and refrigerate for about 30 minutes to firm up.

2. Prepare the Streusel Topping:

- In a medium bowl, combine flour, granulated sugar, melted butter, and ground cinnamon (if using). Mix with a fork until crumbly and well combined. The mixture should resemble coarse crumbs.

3. Assemble and Bake the Streuselplätzchen:

- Preheat your oven to 350°F (175°C). Line baking sheets with parchment paper.
- Scoop tablespoon-sized portions of chilled cookie dough and roll them into balls. Place them 2 inches (5 cm) apart on the prepared baking sheets.
- Flatten each cookie ball slightly with your fingers or the bottom of a glass.
- Sprinkle the streusel topping generously over each cookie, pressing it gently into the dough.

- Bake in the preheated oven for 12-15 minutes, or until the edges of the cookies are golden brown.
- Remove from the oven and let the cookies cool on the baking sheets for a few minutes before transferring them to a wire rack to cool completely.

4. Serve and Enjoy:

- Once cooled, serve these delicious Streuselplätzchen with your favorite hot beverage.
- Store any leftover cookies in an airtight container at room temperature for up to one week.

These Streuselplätzchen are a wonderful treat with their crumbly texture and sweet streusel topping, perfect for any occasion or holiday baking. Enjoy making and sharing them with family and friends!

Lebkuchen (German Gingerbread)

Ingredients:

For the Lebkuchen Dough:

- 2 cups (250g) all-purpose flour
- 1 teaspoon baking powder
- 1/2 teaspoon baking soda
- 1 tablespoon ground ginger
- 1 tablespoon ground cinnamon
- 1/2 teaspoon ground cloves
- 1/2 teaspoon ground nutmeg
- 1/2 teaspoon ground allspice
- Zest of 1 lemon
- Zest of 1 orange
- 1/2 cup (120g) unsalted butter, softened
- 1/2 cup (100g) granulated sugar
- 1/2 cup (120ml) honey
- 1 large egg

For the Glaze:

- 1 cup (120g) powdered sugar
- 2-3 tablespoons lemon juice or milk
- Optional: Candied citrus peel or nuts for decoration

Instructions:

1. Prepare the Lebkuchen Dough:

- In a medium bowl, whisk together flour, baking powder, baking soda, ground ginger, cinnamon, cloves, nutmeg, allspice, lemon zest, and orange zest. Set aside.
- In a large mixing bowl, cream together softened butter and granulated sugar until light and fluffy.
- Add honey and egg to the butter mixture, beating until well combined.
- Gradually add the flour mixture to the wet ingredients, mixing until a smooth dough forms. The dough will be slightly sticky.
- Cover the dough with plastic wrap and refrigerate for at least 1 hour, or overnight, to firm up.

2. Shape and Bake the Lebkuchen:

- Preheat your oven to 350°F (175°C). Line baking sheets with parchment paper.
- On a lightly floured surface, roll out the chilled dough to about 1/4-inch (6mm) thickness.

- Use cookie cutters or a sharp knife to cut out shapes, such as rounds or rectangles, depending on your preference.
- Place the cut-out cookies onto the prepared baking sheets, spacing them about 1 inch (2.5 cm) apart.
- Bake in the preheated oven for 10-12 minutes, or until the edges are lightly browned and the cookies are set.
- Remove from the oven and transfer the cookies to a wire rack to cool completely.

3. Prepare the Glaze:

- In a small bowl, whisk together powdered sugar and lemon juice or milk until smooth. Adjust the consistency by adding more liquid or powdered sugar as needed.

4. Glaze and Decorate the Lebkuchen:

- Once the cookies are completely cooled, spread or drizzle the glaze over the tops of the cookies using a spoon or pastry brush.
- Optionally, decorate the glazed cookies with candied citrus peel or nuts while the glaze is still wet.
- Let the glaze set completely before storing the Lebkuchen in an airtight container at room temperature.

5. Serve and Enjoy:

- Lebkuchen is traditionally enjoyed during the holiday season. Serve these spiced gingerbread cookies with hot tea or mulled wine for a cozy treat.

This recipe yields wonderfully fragrant and flavorful Lebkuchen that captures the essence of German holiday baking. Adjust the spices and decorations according to your taste preferences and enjoy the festive spirit!

Marzipan Kartoffeln (Marzipan Potatoes)

Ingredients:

- 200g marzipan paste
- 1 tablespoon rum or rum flavoring (optional)
- 1/2 teaspoon vanilla extract
- 1/2 cup (50g) powdered sugar (confectioners' sugar)
- 1/4 cup (25g) unsweetened cocoa powder

Instructions:

1. **Prepare the Marzipan Mixture:**
    - In a mixing bowl, crumble the marzipan paste.
    - Add the rum or rum flavoring (if using) and vanilla extract.
    - Knead the mixture until smooth and well combined. If the mixture is too sticky, you can dust your hands lightly with powdered sugar.
2. **Shape the Marzipan Potatoes:**
    - Pinch off small portions of the marzipan mixture and roll them between your palms to form small, irregularly shaped potato-like balls. They should be about the size of small potatoes.
3. **Coat with Cocoa Powder:**
    - In a separate bowl, mix together the powdered sugar and cocoa powder until well combined.
    - Roll each marzipan ball in the cocoa powder mixture until evenly coated. The cocoa powder gives them a realistic "potato" appearance.
4. **Finish and Store:**
    - Place the coated Marzipan Kartoffeln on a baking sheet or plate lined with parchment paper.
    - Let them dry and set at room temperature for at least 1 hour.
5. **Serve and Enjoy:**
    - Once dried and set, transfer the Marzipan Potatoes to an airtight container for storage.
    - They can be enjoyed immediately or stored at room temperature for several days. They also make wonderful edible gifts during the holiday season.

These Marzipan Kartoffeln are a fun and delicious treat that captures the rich almond flavor of marzipan with a hint of cocoa. They are sure to be a hit with friends and family, especially those who appreciate traditional German sweets.

Eiskaffee Torte (Iced Coffee Cake)

Ingredients:

For the Cake:

- 1 1/2 cups (190g) all-purpose flour
- 1 1/2 teaspoons baking powder
- 1/2 teaspoon baking soda
- 1/4 teaspoon salt
- 1/2 cup (120ml) strong brewed coffee, cooled to room temperature
- 1/4 cup (60ml) milk
- 1 teaspoon vanilla extract
- 1/2 cup (115g) unsalted butter, softened
- 1 cup (200g) granulated sugar
- 2 large eggs

For the Coffee Cream Filling:

- 1 cup (240ml) heavy cream, chilled
- 2 tablespoons powdered sugar
- 2 tablespoons instant coffee granules
- 1 tablespoon hot water

For the Coffee Glaze:

- 1 cup (120g) powdered sugar
- 1 tablespoon instant coffee granules
- 2-3 tablespoons milk or cream

Instructions:

1. Prepare the Cake:

- Preheat your oven to 350°F (175°C). Grease and flour a 9-inch (23cm) round cake pan.
- In a medium bowl, whisk together flour, baking powder, baking soda, and salt. Set aside.
- In another bowl, combine brewed coffee, milk, and vanilla extract. Set aside.
- In a large mixing bowl, cream together softened butter and granulated sugar until light and fluffy.
- Add eggs one at a time, beating well after each addition.
- Gradually add the dry ingredients to the butter mixture, alternating with the coffee mixture, beginning and ending with the dry ingredients. Mix until just combined.
- Pour the batter into the prepared cake pan and smooth the top.
- Bake in the preheated oven for 25-30 minutes, or until a toothpick inserted into the center comes out clean.

- Remove from the oven and let the cake cool in the pan for 10 minutes before transferring it to a wire rack to cool completely.

2. Prepare the Coffee Cream Filling:

- In a small bowl, dissolve instant coffee granules in hot water. Let it cool to room temperature.
- In a large mixing bowl, whip chilled heavy cream with powdered sugar until stiff peaks form.
- Gradually fold in the cooled coffee mixture until well combined.

3. Assemble the Eiskaffee Torte:

- Once the cake is completely cooled, carefully slice it horizontally into two even layers.
- Place one cake layer on a serving plate. Spread the coffee cream filling evenly over the top.
- Place the second cake layer on top of the filling.

4. Prepare the Coffee Glaze:

- In a small bowl, whisk together powdered sugar, instant coffee granules, and milk or cream until smooth. Adjust the consistency by adding more milk or powdered sugar as needed.

5. Glaze and Serve:

- Pour the coffee glaze over the top of the cake, allowing it to drip down the sides.
- Optional: Garnish with chocolate shavings or cocoa powder for decoration.
- Refrigerate the Eiskaffee Torte for at least 1 hour before serving to allow the flavors to meld together.

6. Serve and Enjoy:

- Slice and serve chilled. This Eiskaffee Torte is perfect for coffee lovers and makes a delicious dessert for any occasion, especially during warmer weather.

This recipe yields a moist and flavorful cake with a creamy coffee filling and a delicious coffee glaze, capturing the essence of Eiskaffee in a delightful dessert form.

Gugelhupf (Bundt Cake)

Ingredients:

- 2 1/2 cups (300g) all-purpose flour
- 1 tablespoon baking powder
- 1/2 teaspoon salt
- 1 cup (225g) unsalted butter, softened
- 1 1/2 cups (300g) granulated sugar
- 4 large eggs
- 1 teaspoon vanilla extract
- Zest of 1 lemon
- 1/2 cup (120ml) milk

For Dusting (Optional):

- Powdered sugar

Instructions:

1. Prepare the Gugelhupf:

- Preheat your oven to 350°F (175°C). Grease and flour a 10-inch (25cm) Gugelhupf or Bundt cake pan.
- In a medium bowl, whisk together flour, baking powder, and salt. Set aside.
- In a large mixing bowl, cream together softened butter and granulated sugar until light and fluffy.
- Add eggs one at a time, beating well after each addition.
- Stir in vanilla extract and lemon zest.
- Gradually add the flour mixture to the butter mixture, alternating with milk, beginning and ending with the flour mixture. Mix until just combined, being careful not to overmix.

2. Bake the Gugelhupf:

- Pour the batter into the prepared cake pan, spreading it evenly.
- Bake in the preheated oven for 50-60 minutes, or until a toothpick inserted into the center of the cake comes out clean.
- Remove from the oven and let the cake cool in the pan for 10 minutes before transferring it to a wire rack to cool completely.

3. Serve:

- Once cooled, you can dust the Gugelhupf with powdered sugar if desired.
- Slice and serve the Gugelhupf as a delightful treat with coffee or tea.

4. Storage:

- Store any leftover Gugelhupf in an airtight container at room temperature for up to 3 days, or freeze for longer storage.

Enjoy this classic Gugelhupf cake, perfect for any occasion or as a sweet treat with its buttery, tender crumb and subtle lemon flavor!

Kartoffelkuchen (Potato Cake)

Ingredients:

- 1 kg (2.2 lbs) potatoes, peeled and thinly sliced
- 1 onion, thinly sliced
- 150g (5.3 oz) bacon, diced (optional)
- 4 eggs
- 200ml (3/4 cup) milk
- 150g (5.3 oz) Emmental cheese, grated (or any other cheese you prefer)
- Salt and pepper, to taste
- Butter or oil, for greasing

Instructions:

1. **Prepare the Potatoes and Onion:**
    - Preheat your oven to 180°C (350°F).
    - Grease a baking dish (about 9x13 inches or similar size) with butter or oil.
2. **Layer the Potatoes:**
    - Arrange a layer of thinly sliced potatoes on the bottom of the baking dish.
    - Sprinkle with some of the sliced onions and diced bacon (if using).
    - Season lightly with salt and pepper.
3. **Repeat Layers:**
    - Continue layering potatoes, onions, and bacon until all ingredients are used, ending with a layer of potatoes on top.
4. **Prepare the Egg Mixture:**
    - In a bowl, whisk together eggs and milk until well combined.
    - Season with salt and pepper.
5. **Pour Over the Potatoes:**
    - Carefully pour the egg and milk mixture over the layered potatoes in the baking dish. Make sure it evenly coats the top.
6. **Bake:**
    - Sprinkle grated cheese evenly over the top of the potato mixture.
    - Bake in the preheated oven for about 50-60 minutes, or until the potatoes are tender and the top is golden brown and set.
7. **Serve:**
    - Remove from the oven and let it cool slightly before serving.
    - Cut into squares and serve warm as a main dish or a hearty side.

Kartoffelkuchen is a comforting and satisfying dish, perfect for a cozy family meal or a gathering with friends. The layers of potatoes, onions, and cheese baked with eggs create a deliciously savory treat that highlights the flavors of traditional German cuisine. Enjoy!

Rhabarberkuchen (Rhubarb Cake)

Ingredients:

For the Cake Batter:

- 1 1/2 cups (190g) all-purpose flour
- 1 1/2 teaspoons baking powder
- 1/2 teaspoon salt
- 1/2 cup (115g) unsalted butter, softened
- 3/4 cup (150g) granulated sugar
- 2 large eggs
- 1 teaspoon vanilla extract
- 1/2 cup (120ml) milk

For the Rhubarb Topping:

- 3 cups (about 350g) fresh rhubarb, washed and cut into 1-inch pieces
- 1/2 cup (100g) granulated sugar
- 1 tablespoon cornstarch

For the Streusel Topping (optional):

- 1/2 cup (65g) all-purpose flour
- 1/4 cup (50g) granulated sugar
- 1/4 cup (55g) unsalted butter, cold and cubed

Instructions:

1. Prepare the Rhubarb:

- Preheat your oven to 350°F (175°C). Grease and flour a 9x13-inch baking dish or line it with parchment paper.
- In a medium bowl, toss the rhubarb pieces with sugar and cornstarch until evenly coated. Set aside.

2. Make the Cake Batter:

- In a separate bowl, whisk together flour, baking powder, and salt. Set aside.
- In a large mixing bowl, cream together softened butter and sugar until light and fluffy.
- Add eggs one at a time, beating well after each addition. Mix in vanilla extract.
- Gradually add the flour mixture to the butter mixture, alternating with milk, beginning and ending with the flour mixture. Mix until just combined.

3. Assemble the Cake:

- Spread the cake batter evenly into the prepared baking dish.

- Evenly distribute the rhubarb mixture over the cake batter.

4. Optional Streusel Topping:

- If using streusel topping, combine flour and sugar in a bowl. Cut in cold cubed butter using a pastry cutter or your fingers until mixture resembles coarse crumbs. Sprinkle evenly over the rhubarb layer.

5. Bake:

- Bake in the preheated oven for 45-50 minutes, or until the cake is golden brown and a toothpick inserted into the center comes out clean.

6. Serve:

- Let the Rhubarb Cake cool in the pan for 10-15 minutes before slicing and serving.
- Serve warm or at room temperature. Optionally, top with a dollop of whipped cream or a scoop of vanilla ice cream.

This Rhubarb Cake is a wonderful way to enjoy the tart flavor of rhubarb in a moist and tender cake. It's perfect for afternoon tea or as a delightful dessert after a springtime meal. Enjoy!

Butterkuchen (Butter Cake)

Ingredients:

For the Cake:

- 2 cups (250g) all-purpose flour
- 1/2 cup (100g) granulated sugar
- 1/2 teaspoon salt
- 1 tablespoon active dry yeast
- 3/4 cup (180ml) lukewarm milk
- 1/4 cup (60g) unsalted butter, softened
- 1 large egg

For the Topping:

- 1/2 cup (115g) unsalted butter, melted
- 1/2 cup (100g) granulated sugar
- 1 tablespoon vanilla sugar or 1 teaspoon vanilla extract
- 1/2 cup (50g) sliced almonds (optional)

Instructions:

1. Prepare the Dough:

- In a large mixing bowl, combine flour, sugar, and salt.
- In a small bowl, dissolve yeast in lukewarm milk. Let it sit for 5-10 minutes until foamy.
- Make a well in the center of the dry ingredients and pour in the yeast mixture, softened butter, and egg.
- Mix everything together until a soft dough forms. You can use a stand mixer with a dough hook attachment or knead by hand on a lightly floured surface.
- Knead the dough for about 5-7 minutes until smooth and elastic. Shape it into a ball.
- Place the dough back into the bowl, cover with a clean kitchen towel, and let it rise in a warm place for about 1 hour, or until doubled in size.

2. Preheat the Oven and Prepare the Topping:

- Preheat your oven to 375°F (190°C). Grease a 9x13-inch baking dish or line it with parchment paper.
- In a small bowl, mix together melted butter, granulated sugar, and vanilla sugar or vanilla extract.

3. Shape and Bake the Cake:

- Punch down the risen dough and transfer it to the prepared baking dish.

- Gently press and spread the dough evenly into the pan using your fingers, making sure it reaches all corners.
- Brush the butter-sugar mixture generously over the surface of the dough. Sprinkle sliced almonds evenly on top if desired.
- Let the Butterkuchen rise again in a warm place for about 15-20 minutes.

4. Bake and Serve:

- Bake in the preheated oven for 20-25 minutes, or until the cake is golden brown and cooked through.
- Remove from the oven and let it cool slightly in the pan. Optionally, dust with powdered sugar before serving.
- Cut into squares or rectangles and serve warm or at room temperature.

5. Enjoy:

- Butterkuchen is best enjoyed fresh on the day it's made, but leftovers can be stored in an airtight container at room temperature for up to 2 days.

This Butterkuchen recipe yields a deliciously soft and buttery cake with a sweet topping that caramelizes beautifully during baking. It's a perfect treat to enjoy for breakfast, brunch, or dessert, showcasing the simplicity and richness of traditional German baking.

Spaghettieis Torte (Spaghetti Ice Cream Cake)

Ingredients:

For the Cake Base:

- 1 store-bought sponge cake or vanilla cake, sliced into layers (or homemade cake if preferred)

For the Ice Cream Layers:

- 1 liter of vanilla ice cream, softened
- 1 liter of strawberry or raspberry sorbet, softened

For the Toppings:

- 1 cup strawberry sauce or raspberry sauce (store-bought or homemade)
- White chocolate shavings or grated white chocolate
- Fresh strawberries, for garnish (optional)

Instructions:

1. Prepare the Cake Base:

- If using store-bought cake, slice it horizontally into 2 or 3 even layers. Alternatively, bake and cool your own vanilla sponge cake.
- Line a springform pan with parchment paper or plastic wrap for easy removal.
- Place the bottom layer of cake in the prepared pan.

2. Assemble the Ice Cream Layers:

- In a large mixing bowl, soften the vanilla ice cream until it's easy to spread but not melted.
- Spread a layer of softened vanilla ice cream evenly over the cake layer in the pan. Smooth the top with a spatula.
- Place the cake in the freezer for about 30 minutes to set the ice cream layer.
- Once the vanilla ice cream layer is firm, spread a layer of softened strawberry or raspberry sorbet evenly over the vanilla ice cream layer. Smooth the top.
- Return the cake to the freezer for another 30 minutes to set the sorbet layer.

3. Final Assembly:

- Spread another layer of softened vanilla ice cream over the sorbet layer. Smooth the top evenly.
- Place the final layer of cake on top of the vanilla ice cream layer, pressing gently to adhere.

4. Finish with Toppings:

- Spread strawberry sauce or raspberry sauce over the top layer of cake, mimicking the look of spaghetti sauce.
- Sprinkle generous amounts of white chocolate shavings or grated white chocolate over the sauce to resemble Parmesan cheese.
- Optionally, garnish with fresh strawberries or other berries for decoration.

5. Freeze and Serve:

- Cover the Spaghettieis Torte with plastic wrap and place it in the freezer for at least 4 hours, or preferably overnight, to firm up and set completely.
- Before serving, remove the cake from the springform pan and transfer it to a serving platter.
- Slice and serve the Spaghettieis Torte chilled. Enjoy the fun and delicious flavors reminiscent of the popular German ice cream dessert!

This Spaghettieis Torte is a creative twist on a beloved treat, combining the elements of cake, ice cream, and fruity sauce into a delightful and visually appealing dessert that's perfect for special occasions or summer gatherings.

Holunderblütenkuchen (Elderflower Cake)

Ingredients:

For the Cake:

- 1 1/2 cups (190g) all-purpose flour
- 1 1/2 teaspoons baking powder
- 1/2 teaspoon salt
- 1/2 cup (115g) unsalted butter, softened
- 1 cup (200g) granulated sugar
- 2 large eggs
- 1 teaspoon vanilla extract
- Zest of 1 lemon
- 1/2 cup (120ml) milk
- 2-3 tablespoons elderflower syrup or elderflower cordial (adjust to taste)

For the Elderflower Glaze:

- 1 cup (120g) powdered sugar
- 2-3 tablespoons elderflower syrup or elderflower cordial
- Fresh elderflowers for decoration (optional)

Instructions:

1. Prepare the Cake:

- Preheat your oven to 350°F (175°C). Grease and flour a 9-inch (23cm) round cake pan.
- In a medium bowl, whisk together flour, baking powder, and salt. Set aside.
- In a large mixing bowl, cream together softened butter and granulated sugar until light and fluffy.
- Add eggs one at a time, beating well after each addition. Mix in vanilla extract and lemon zest.
- Gradually add the dry ingredients to the butter mixture, alternating with milk, beginning and ending with the dry ingredients. Mix until just combined.
- Stir in elderflower syrup or elderflower cordial until well incorporated, adjusting to taste.
- Pour the batter into the prepared cake pan, spreading it evenly.

2. Bake the Cake:

- Bake in the preheated oven for 25-30 minutes, or until a toothpick inserted into the center comes out clean.
- Remove from the oven and let the cake cool in the pan for 10 minutes before transferring it to a wire rack to cool completely.

3. Prepare the Elderflower Glaze:

- In a small bowl, whisk together powdered sugar and elderflower syrup or elderflower cordial until smooth. Adjust the consistency by adding more syrup or powdered sugar as needed.

4. Glaze and Decorate:

- Once the cake has cooled completely, drizzle the elderflower glaze over the top of the cake, allowing it to drip down the sides.
- Optionally, decorate with fresh elderflowers on top for an elegant touch.

5. Serve and Enjoy:

- Slice and serve the Elderflower Cake as a delightful dessert or afternoon treat. The floral notes of elderflower combined with the moist and tender cake make for a refreshing and aromatic experience.

This Elderflower Cake is perfect for celebrating the flavors of spring and summer, capturing the essence of elderflower in a beautifully presented dessert. Enjoy its delicate floral taste with friends and family!

Kalter Hund (No-Bake Chocolate Biscuit Cake)

Ingredients:

- 400g (about 14 oz) of plain biscuits (such as butter biscuits or tea biscuits)
- 200g (7 oz) dark chocolate
- 200g (7 oz) milk chocolate
- 200g (7 oz) unsalted butter
- 1/2 cup (120ml) heavy cream
- 1 teaspoon vanilla extract
- Optional: 1-2 tablespoons rum or rum flavoring (to taste)
- Chocolate sprinkles or grated chocolate for decoration

Instructions:

1. Prepare the Biscuits:

- Line a loaf pan with parchment paper or plastic wrap, leaving some overhang for easy removal later.
- Arrange a layer of biscuits to cover the bottom of the pan. Break the biscuits if needed to fit.

2. Make the Chocolate Mixture:

- In a heatproof bowl, combine the dark chocolate, milk chocolate, and butter. Place the bowl over a pot of simmering water (double boiler method) and melt the chocolate and butter together, stirring occasionally until smooth.
- Once melted, remove from heat and stir in the heavy cream, vanilla extract, and rum (if using). Mix until well combined and smooth.

3. Assemble the Cake:

- Pour a layer of the chocolate mixture over the layer of biscuits in the loaf pan, spreading it evenly with a spatula.
- Add another layer of biscuits over the chocolate mixture. Continue alternating layers of biscuits and chocolate mixture until you reach the top of the pan, finishing with a layer of chocolate mixture on top.

4. Chill the Cake:

- Cover the loaf pan with plastic wrap and refrigerate for at least 4 hours, or preferably overnight, until the cake is firm and set.

5. Serve:

- Once chilled and set, lift the Kalter Hund out of the loaf pan using the parchment paper or plastic wrap overhang.
- Optionally, decorate with chocolate sprinkles or grated chocolate on top.
- Slice and serve the Kalter Hund chilled. It should have a firm, fudgy texture with layers of biscuits and chocolate.

6. Enjoy:

- Kalter Hund is best enjoyed cold, making it a refreshing and indulgent dessert. Serve it as slices or squares, and store any leftovers in the refrigerator.

This no-bake chocolate biscuit cake is a favorite for its simplicity and rich chocolate flavor, perfect for gatherings or simply satisfying a sweet tooth with minimal effort.

Sonntagskuchen (Sunday Cake)

Ingredients:

For the Cake:

- 2 cups (250g) all-purpose flour
- 2 teaspoons baking powder
- 1/2 teaspoon salt
- 1 cup (225g) unsalted butter, softened
- 1 cup (200g) granulated sugar
- 4 large eggs
- 1 teaspoon vanilla extract
- Zest of 1 lemon (optional)
- 1/2 cup (120ml) milk

For the Glaze:

- 1 cup (120g) powdered sugar
- 2-3 tablespoons lemon juice (or milk for a different flavor)

Optional Toppings:

- Sliced almonds, powdered sugar, or fresh berries for decoration

Instructions:

1. Prepare the Cake:

- Preheat your oven to 350°F (175°C). Grease and flour a 9-inch (23cm) round cake pan or line it with parchment paper.
- In a medium bowl, whisk together flour, baking powder, and salt. Set aside.
- In a large mixing bowl, cream together softened butter and granulated sugar until light and fluffy.
- Add eggs one at a time, beating well after each addition. Mix in vanilla extract and lemon zest if using.
- Gradually add the dry ingredients to the butter mixture, alternating with milk, beginning and ending with the dry ingredients. Mix until just combined.
- Pour the batter into the prepared cake pan, spreading it evenly.

2. Bake the Cake:

- Bake in the preheated oven for 30-35 minutes, or until a toothpick inserted into the center comes out clean.
- Remove from the oven and let the cake cool in the pan for 10 minutes before transferring it to a wire rack to cool completely.

3. Prepare the Glaze:

- In a small bowl, whisk together powdered sugar and lemon juice (or milk) until smooth. Adjust the consistency by adding more powdered sugar or liquid as needed.

4. Glaze and Decorate:

- Once the cake has cooled completely, place it on a serving plate or cake stand.
- Drizzle the glaze over the top of the cake, allowing it to drip down the sides.
- Optionally, decorate with sliced almonds, powdered sugar, or fresh berries on top.

5. Serve and Enjoy:

- Slice and serve the Sonntagskuchen as a delicious treat for Sunday brunch or afternoon tea.
- Store any leftovers in an airtight container at room temperature for up to 3 days, or refrigerate for longer storage.

This Sonntagskuchen recipe yields a moist and flavorful cake with a hint of citrus, perfect for sharing with family and friends on a relaxed Sunday afternoon. Enjoy its simplicity and comforting flavors!

Zitronenkuchen (Lemon Cake)

Ingredients:

For the Cake:

- 1 1/2 cups (190g) all-purpose flour
- 2 teaspoons baking powder
- 1/2 teaspoon salt
- 1 cup (200g) granulated sugar
- 1/2 cup (120ml) vegetable oil or melted butter
- 3 large eggs
- Zest of 2 lemons
- 1/4 cup (60ml) fresh lemon juice
- 1/2 cup (120ml) buttermilk (or substitute with 1/2 cup milk mixed with 1/2 tablespoon lemon juice or vinegar, let sit for 5 minutes)
- 1 teaspoon vanilla extract

For the Lemon Glaze:

- 1 cup (120g) powdered sugar
- 2-3 tablespoons fresh lemon juice

Instructions:

1. Prepare the Cake:

- Preheat your oven to 350°F (175°C). Grease and flour a 9x5-inch (23x13cm) loaf pan or line it with parchment paper.
- In a medium bowl, whisk together flour, baking powder, and salt. Set aside.
- In a large mixing bowl, whisk together granulated sugar, vegetable oil or melted butter, eggs, lemon zest, lemon juice, buttermilk, and vanilla extract until smooth.
- Gradually add the dry ingredients to the wet ingredients, mixing until just combined. Be careful not to overmix.
- Pour the batter into the prepared loaf pan, spreading it evenly.

2. Bake the Cake:

- Bake in the preheated oven for 45-55 minutes, or until a toothpick inserted into the center of the cake comes out clean.
- Remove from the oven and let the cake cool in the pan for 10-15 minutes before transferring it to a wire rack to cool completely.

3. Prepare the Lemon Glaze:

- In a small bowl, whisk together powdered sugar and fresh lemon juice until smooth. Adjust the consistency by adding more lemon juice or powdered sugar as needed.

4. Glaze and Serve:

- Once the cake has cooled completely, place it on a serving plate or cake stand.
- Drizzle the lemon glaze over the top of the cake, allowing it to drip down the sides.

5. Optional Decoration:

- Garnish with extra lemon zest on top for added freshness, if desired.

6. Serve and Enjoy:

- Slice and serve the Zitronenkuchen as a delightful dessert or afternoon treat, paired with tea or coffee.
- Store any leftovers in an airtight container at room temperature for up to 3 days, or refrigerate for longer freshness.

This Zitronenkuchen recipe yields a moist and flavorful cake with a burst of lemon flavor in every bite. It's perfect for any occasion and sure to brighten up your day with its citrusy goodness!

Schmandkuchen (Sour Cream Cake)

Ingredients:

For the Cake:

- 2 cups (250g) all-purpose flour
- 1 1/2 teaspoons baking powder
- 1/2 teaspoon baking soda
- 1/4 teaspoon salt
- 1/2 cup (115g) unsalted butter, softened
- 1 cup (200g) granulated sugar
- 2 large eggs
- 1 teaspoon vanilla extract
- 1 cup (240g) sour cream

For the Streusel Topping:

- 1/2 cup (100g) granulated sugar
- 1/2 cup (60g) all-purpose flour
- 1/4 cup (60g) unsalted butter, cold and cubed
- 1 teaspoon ground cinnamon (optional)

Instructions:

1. Preheat the Oven:

- Preheat your oven to 350°F (175°C). Grease and flour a 9-inch (23cm) springform pan or line it with parchment paper.

2. Make the Streusel Topping:

- In a small bowl, combine granulated sugar, flour, and ground cinnamon (if using).
- Cut in cold cubed butter using a pastry cutter or fork until the mixture resembles coarse crumbs. Set aside.

3. Prepare the Cake Batter:

- In a medium bowl, whisk together flour, baking powder, baking soda, and salt. Set aside.
- In a large mixing bowl, cream together softened butter and granulated sugar until light and fluffy.
- Add eggs one at a time, beating well after each addition. Mix in vanilla extract.
- Gradually add the dry ingredients to the butter mixture, alternating with sour cream, beginning and ending with the dry ingredients. Mix until just combined.

4. Assemble and Bake:

- Spread the cake batter evenly into the prepared springform pan, smoothing the top with a spatula.
- Sprinkle the streusel topping evenly over the cake batter, covering the entire surface.

5. Bake the Cake:

- Bake in the preheated oven for 35-40 minutes, or until a toothpick inserted into the center of the cake comes out clean.
- Remove from the oven and let the cake cool in the pan on a wire rack for 10-15 minutes.
- Release the sides of the springform pan and let the cake cool completely on the wire rack.

6. Serve and Enjoy:

- Once cooled, slice and serve the Schmandkuchen at room temperature. It's delicious on its own or served with a dollop of whipped cream or a scoop of vanilla ice cream.
- Store any leftovers in an airtight container in the refrigerator for up to 3 days. The flavors may even improve the next day!

This Schmandkuchen recipe yields a tender and flavorful cake with a delightful streusel topping, perfect for enjoying with coffee or tea as a classic German dessert.

Beerenkuchen (Berry Cake)

Ingredients:

For the Cake:

- 1 1/2 cups (190g) all-purpose flour
- 1 1/2 teaspoons baking powder
- 1/2 teaspoon salt
- 1/2 cup (115g) unsalted butter, softened
- 3/4 cup (150g) granulated sugar
- 2 large eggs
- 1 teaspoon vanilla extract
- 1/2 cup (120ml) milk

For the Berry Topping:

- 2 cups mixed fresh berries (such as strawberries, raspberries, blueberries, or blackberries), washed and hulled if needed
- 2 tablespoons granulated sugar
- 1 tablespoon lemon juice

For the Streusel Topping (optional):

- 1/4 cup (50g) granulated sugar
- 1/4 cup (30g) all-purpose flour
- 2 tablespoons unsalted butter, cold and cubed

Instructions:

1. Preheat the Oven and Prepare the Pan:

- Preheat your oven to 350°F (175°C). Grease and flour a 9-inch (23cm) round cake pan or line it with parchment paper.

2. Prepare the Berry Topping:

- In a bowl, toss the mixed fresh berries with granulated sugar and lemon juice. Set aside to macerate while preparing the cake batter.

3. Make the Cake Batter:

- In a medium bowl, whisk together flour, baking powder, and salt. Set aside.
- In a large mixing bowl, cream together softened butter and granulated sugar until light and fluffy.
- Add eggs one at a time, beating well after each addition. Mix in vanilla extract.

- Gradually add the dry ingredients to the butter mixture, alternating with milk, beginning and ending with the dry ingredients. Mix until just combined.

4. Assemble and Bake the Cake:

- Spread the cake batter evenly into the prepared cake pan, smoothing the top with a spatula.
- Arrange the macerated berries evenly over the top of the cake batter.

5. Optional Streusel Topping:

- If using the streusel topping, combine granulated sugar and flour in a bowl. Cut in cold cubed butter using a pastry cutter or fork until the mixture resembles coarse crumbs. Sprinkle evenly over the berries.

6. Bake the Cake:

- Bake in the preheated oven for 30-35 minutes, or until a toothpick inserted into the center of the cake comes out clean.
- Remove from the oven and let the cake cool in the pan on a wire rack for 10-15 minutes.
- Release the sides of the cake pan and let the cake cool completely on the wire rack.

7. Serve and Enjoy:

- Once cooled, slice and serve the Beerenkuchen at room temperature. It's delicious on its own or served with a dollop of whipped cream or a scoop of vanilla ice cream.
- Store any leftovers in an airtight container in the refrigerator for up to 3 days.

This Beerenkuchen recipe highlights the natural sweetness of fresh berries, making it a perfect summer dessert or a delightful treat for any occasion. Enjoy the burst of flavors with each bite!

Kirschtorte (Cherry Cake)

Ingredients:

For the Cake:

- 1 1/2 cups (190g) all-purpose flour
- 1 1/2 teaspoons baking powder
- 1/2 teaspoon baking soda
- 1/4 teaspoon salt
- 1/2 cup (115g) unsalted butter, softened
- 1 cup (200g) granulated sugar
- 2 large eggs
- 1 teaspoon vanilla extract
- 1/2 cup (120ml) buttermilk (or substitute with 1/2 cup milk mixed with 1/2 tablespoon lemon juice or vinegar, let sit for 5 minutes)

For the Cherry Filling:

- 2 cups fresh cherries, pitted and halved (or canned/jarred cherries, drained)
- 1/4 cup (50g) granulated sugar
- 1 tablespoon cornstarch
- 1 tablespoon lemon juice

For the Whipped Cream Frosting:

- 1 1/2 cups (360ml) heavy cream, chilled
- 1/4 cup (30g) powdered sugar
- 1 teaspoon vanilla extract
- Fresh cherries for decoration (optional)

Instructions:

1. Preheat the Oven and Prepare the Pan:

- Preheat your oven to 350°F (175°C). Grease and flour two 8-inch (20cm) round cake pans or line them with parchment paper.

2. Make the Cake Batter:

- In a medium bowl, whisk together flour, baking powder, baking soda, and salt. Set aside.
- In a large mixing bowl, cream together softened butter and granulated sugar until light and fluffy.
- Add eggs one at a time, beating well after each addition. Mix in vanilla extract.
- Gradually add the dry ingredients to the butter mixture, alternating with buttermilk, beginning and ending with the dry ingredients. Mix until just combined.

- Divide the batter evenly between the prepared cake pans, spreading it evenly with a spatula.

3. Bake the Cakes:

- Bake in the preheated oven for 25-30 minutes, or until a toothpick inserted into the center of the cakes comes out clean.
- Remove from the oven and let the cakes cool in the pans on a wire rack for 10-15 minutes. Then, remove the cakes from the pans and let them cool completely on the wire rack.

4. Make the Cherry Filling:

- In a saucepan, combine fresh cherries, granulated sugar, cornstarch, and lemon juice. Cook over medium heat, stirring constantly, until the mixture thickens and the cherries release their juices, about 5-7 minutes. Remove from heat and let cool completely.

5. Prepare the Whipped Cream Frosting:

- In a chilled mixing bowl, whip heavy cream, powdered sugar, and vanilla extract until stiff peaks form.

6. Assemble the Kirschtorte:

- Place one cooled cake layer on a serving plate or cake stand.
- Spread half of the whipped cream frosting evenly over the cake layer.
- Spoon the cooled cherry filling over the whipped cream layer, spreading it evenly.
- Top with the second cake layer. Spread the remaining whipped cream frosting over the top and sides of the cake.
- Optionally, decorate with fresh cherries on top.

7. Chill and Serve:

- Chill the Kirschtorte in the refrigerator for at least 1 hour before serving to allow the flavors to meld.
- Slice and serve the Kirschtorte chilled. Enjoy the combination of moist cake layers, sweet cherry filling, and light whipped cream frosting!

This Kirschtorte recipe captures the essence of a classic German Cherry Cake, perfect for celebrating with family and friends, especially during cherry season.

Aprikosenkuchen (Apricot Cake)

Ingredients:

For the Cake:

- 1 1/2 cups (190g) all-purpose flour
- 1 1/2 teaspoons baking powder
- 1/2 teaspoon salt
- 1/2 cup (115g) unsalted butter, softened
- 3/4 cup (150g) granulated sugar
- 2 large eggs
- 1 teaspoon vanilla extract
- 1/2 cup (120ml) milk

For the Apricot Topping:

- 4-5 fresh apricots, halved and pitted (about 1 pound or 450g)
- 1/4 cup (50g) granulated sugar
- 1 tablespoon lemon juice
- 1 tablespoon apricot jam or preserves

Optional Streusel Topping:

- 1/4 cup (50g) granulated sugar
- 1/4 cup (30g) all-purpose flour
- 2 tablespoons unsalted butter, cold and cubed

Instructions:

1. Preheat the Oven and Prepare the Pan:

- Preheat your oven to 350°F (175°C). Grease and flour a 9-inch (23cm) round cake pan or line it with parchment paper.

2. Make the Cake Batter:

- In a medium bowl, whisk together flour, baking powder, and salt. Set aside.
- In a large mixing bowl, cream together softened butter and granulated sugar until light and fluffy.
- Add eggs one at a time, beating well after each addition. Mix in vanilla extract.
- Gradually add the dry ingredients to the butter mixture, alternating with milk, beginning and ending with the dry ingredients. Mix until just combined.
- Spread the cake batter evenly into the prepared cake pan, smoothing the top with a spatula.

3. Prepare the Apricot Topping:

- Arrange the apricot halves, cut side up, evenly over the cake batter in the pan.
- In a small bowl, mix together granulated sugar and lemon juice. Drizzle the mixture evenly over the apricots.
- Warm the apricot jam or preserves slightly in the microwave or on the stovetop until it becomes more liquid. Brush the apricot jam over the apricots to glaze them.

4. Optional Streusel Topping (if desired):

- Combine granulated sugar and flour in a bowl. Cut in cold cubed butter using a pastry cutter or fork until the mixture resembles coarse crumbs. Sprinkle evenly over the apricots.

5. Bake the Cake:

- Bake in the preheated oven for 35-40 minutes, or until a toothpick inserted into the center of the cake comes out clean.
- Remove from the oven and let the cake cool in the pan on a wire rack for 10-15 minutes.
- Release the sides of the cake pan and let the cake cool completely on the wire rack.

6. Serve and Enjoy:

- Once cooled, slice and serve the Aprikosenkuchen at room temperature. It's delicious on its own or served with a dollop of whipped cream or vanilla ice cream.
- Store any leftovers in an airtight container in the refrigerator for up to 3 days.

This Aprikosenkuchen recipe captures the essence of summer with its fresh apricot topping and moist cake base, making it a perfect dessert for any occasion. Enjoy the fruity sweetness and delightful flavors!

Sauerkirsch Streuselkuchen (Sour Cherry Crumb Cake)

Ingredients:

For the Cake:

- 2 cups (250g) all-purpose flour
- 1 teaspoon baking powder
- 1/2 teaspoon baking soda
- 1/4 teaspoon salt
- 1/2 cup (115g) unsalted butter, softened
- 3/4 cup (150g) granulated sugar
- 2 large eggs
- 1 teaspoon vanilla extract
- 1/2 cup (120ml) sour cream or plain Greek yogurt

For the Sour Cherry Filling:

- 3 cups pitted sour cherries (fresh or canned, drained)
- 1/4 cup (50g) granulated sugar
- 1 tablespoon cornstarch
- 1 tablespoon lemon juice

For the Streusel Topping:

- 1/2 cup (100g) granulated sugar
- 1/2 cup (60g) all-purpose flour
- 1/4 cup (60g) unsalted butter, cold and cubed
- 1/2 teaspoon ground cinnamon (optional)

Instructions:

1. Preheat the Oven and Prepare the Pan:

- Preheat your oven to 350°F (175°C). Grease and flour a 9x13-inch (23x33cm) baking pan or line it with parchment paper.

2. Make the Streusel Topping:

- In a bowl, combine granulated sugar, flour, and ground cinnamon (if using).
- Cut in cold cubed butter using a pastry cutter or fork until the mixture resembles coarse crumbs. Set aside.

3. Prepare the Sour Cherry Filling:

- In a saucepan, combine pitted sour cherries, granulated sugar, cornstarch, and lemon juice. Cook over medium heat, stirring constantly, until the mixture thickens and the cherries release their juices, about 5-7 minutes. Remove from heat and let cool slightly.

4. Make the Cake Batter:

- In a medium bowl, whisk together flour, baking powder, baking soda, and salt. Set aside.
- In a large mixing bowl, cream together softened butter and granulated sugar until light and fluffy.
- Add eggs one at a time, beating well after each addition. Mix in vanilla extract.
- Gradually add the dry ingredients to the butter mixture, alternating with sour cream or yogurt, beginning and ending with the dry ingredients. Mix until just combined.

5. Assemble the Cake:

- Spread the cake batter evenly into the prepared baking pan, using a spatula to smooth the top.
- Spread the cooled sour cherry filling evenly over the cake batter.
- Sprinkle the streusel topping evenly over the sour cherry filling, covering the entire surface.

6. Bake the Cake:

- Bake in the preheated oven for 40-45 minutes, or until the cake is golden brown and a toothpick inserted into the center comes out clean.
- Remove from the oven and let the cake cool in the pan on a wire rack for 15-20 minutes.

7. Serve and Enjoy:

- Once cooled slightly, slice and serve the Sauerkirsch Streuselkuchen warm or at room temperature. It pairs wonderfully with a cup of coffee or tea.
- Store any leftovers in an airtight container at room temperature for up to 3 days.

This Sour Cherry Crumb Cake is a delightful treat with its tender cake base, juicy sour cherry filling, and buttery crumb topping. Enjoy the sweet-tart flavors in every bite.

Kirschschnitten (Cherry Slices)

Ingredients:

For the Shortcrust Pastry:

- 2 cups (250g) all-purpose flour
- 1/2 cup (100g) granulated sugar
- 1/4 teaspoon salt
- 1 cup (225g) unsalted butter, cold and cut into small cubes
- 1 large egg yolk
- 2-3 tablespoons cold water

For the Cherry Filling:

- 2 cups pitted cherries (fresh or canned, drained)
- 1/4 cup (50g) granulated sugar
- 1 tablespoon cornstarch
- 1 tablespoon lemon juice

For the Glaze:

- 1/2 cup (60g) powdered sugar
- 1-2 tablespoons milk or water
- 1/2 teaspoon vanilla extract

Instructions:

1. Make the Shortcrust Pastry:

- In a large mixing bowl, combine flour, sugar, and salt. Add the cold butter cubes and rub them into the flour mixture with your fingertips until it resembles coarse crumbs.
- Add the egg yolk and cold water, a tablespoon at a time, mixing with a fork or pastry cutter until the dough just begins to come together. Gather the dough into a ball, flatten into a disc, wrap in plastic wrap, and refrigerate for at least 30 minutes.

2. Prepare the Cherry Filling:

- In a saucepan, combine pitted cherries, granulated sugar, cornstarch, and lemon juice. Cook over medium heat, stirring constantly, until the mixture thickens and the cherries release their juices, about 5-7 minutes. Remove from heat and let cool completely.

3. Preheat the Oven and Prepare the Pan:

- Preheat your oven to 350°F (175°C). Line a 9x13-inch (23x33cm) baking pan with parchment paper, leaving an overhang on the sides for easy removal.

4. Roll Out the Pastry:

- On a lightly floured surface, roll out the chilled pastry dough into a rectangle slightly larger than the baking pan. Carefully transfer the rolled-out dough to the prepared baking pan, pressing it evenly into the bottom and up the sides. Trim any excess dough if necessary.

5. Assemble the Kirschschnitten:

- Spread the cooled cherry filling evenly over the pastry base.

6. Bake the Kirschschnitten:

- Bake in the preheated oven for 25-30 minutes, or until the pastry is golden brown and the filling is set.

7. Make the Glaze:

- In a small bowl, whisk together powdered sugar, milk or water, and vanilla extract until smooth and drizzle consistency.

8. Finish and Serve:

- Remove the Kirschschnitten from the oven and let cool completely in the pan on a wire rack.
- Once cooled, drizzle the glaze over the top. Allow the glaze to set before cutting the Kirschschnitten into slices.

9. Serve and Enjoy:

- Serve the Kirschschnitten slices at room temperature. They are delightful on their own or served with a dollop of whipped cream or a scoop of vanilla ice cream.
- Store any leftovers in an airtight container in the refrigerator for up to 3 days.

These Kirschschnitten are a wonderful treat that showcases the sweet-tart flavors of cherries encased in a buttery pastry, perfect for enjoying with coffee or tea as a delightful German dessert.

Schokoladenkuchen (Chocolate Cake)

Ingredients:

For the Cake:

- 1 3/4 cups (220g) all-purpose flour
- 1 1/2 cups (300g) granulated sugar
- 3/4 cup (65g) unsweetened cocoa powder
- 1 1/2 teaspoons baking powder
- 1 1/2 teaspoons baking soda
- 1 teaspoon salt
- 2 large eggs
- 1 cup (240ml) buttermilk
- 1/2 cup (120ml) vegetable oil
- 2 teaspoons vanilla extract
- 1 cup (240ml) boiling water

For the Chocolate Ganache (optional):

- 1 cup (240ml) heavy cream
- 8 ounces (225g) semisweet or bittersweet chocolate, chopped
- 1 tablespoon unsalted butter (optional, for shine)

Instructions:

1. Preheat the Oven and Prepare the Pan:

- Preheat your oven to 350°F (175°C). Grease and flour two 9-inch (23cm) round cake pans or line them with parchment paper.

2. Make the Cake Batter:

- In a large mixing bowl, whisk together flour, sugar, cocoa powder, baking powder, baking soda, and salt.
- Add eggs, buttermilk, vegetable oil, and vanilla extract. Beat on medium speed for about 2 minutes until well combined.
- Gradually stir in boiling water until the batter is smooth. The batter will be thin, but that's normal.

3. Bake the Cake:

- Pour the batter evenly into the prepared cake pans.
- Bake for 30 to 35 minutes, or until a toothpick inserted into the center comes out clean.
- Remove from the oven and let the cakes cool in the pans for 10 minutes before transferring them to a wire rack to cool completely.

4. Make the Chocolate Ganache (optional):

- Heat the heavy cream in a small saucepan over medium heat until it just begins to boil.
- Place the chopped chocolate in a heatproof bowl. Pour the hot cream over the chocolate and let it sit for 1-2 minutes.
- Stir the chocolate and cream mixture gently until the chocolate is melted and smooth. If desired, stir in butter for extra shine.

5. Assemble the Cake:

- Once the cakes are completely cooled, place one cake layer on a serving plate or cake stand.
- Spread a layer of chocolate ganache on top of the first cake layer (if using).
- Place the second cake layer on top. Spread the remaining ganache over the top and sides of the cake.

6. Serve and Enjoy:

- Slice and serve the Schokoladenkuchen at room temperature. It's delicious on its own or served with whipped cream or vanilla ice cream.
- Store any leftovers in an airtight container in the refrigerator for up to 3 days.

This Schokoladenkuchen recipe yields a rich, moist chocolate cake that is sure to satisfy any chocolate lover's cravings. Enjoy this classic German dessert for birthdays, celebrations, or any special occasion!

Zupfkuchen (German Chocolate Marble Cake)

Ingredients:

For the Dough:

- 2 cups (250g) all-purpose flour
- 1 teaspoon baking powder
- 1/2 teaspoon baking soda
- 1/4 teaspoon salt
- 3/4 cup (170g) unsalted butter, softened
- 1 cup (200g) granulated sugar
- 1 large egg
- 1 teaspoon vanilla extract

For the Chocolate Quark Filling:

- 14 ounces (400g) quark or cream cheese, at room temperature
- 1/2 cup (100g) granulated sugar
- 1 large egg
- 1 teaspoon vanilla extract
- 1/4 cup (30g) unsweetened cocoa powder

For the Streusel Topping:

- 1/4 cup (50g) granulated sugar
- 1/4 cup (30g) all-purpose flour
- 2 tablespoons unsalted butter, cold and cubed
- 1/4 cup (30g) sliced almonds (optional, for topping)

Instructions:

1. Preheat the Oven and Prepare the Pan:

- Preheat your oven to 350°F (175°C). Grease and flour a 9-inch (23cm) springform pan or line it with parchment paper.

2. Make the Dough:

- In a medium bowl, whisk together flour, baking powder, baking soda, and salt. Set aside.
- In a large mixing bowl, cream together softened butter and granulated sugar until light and fluffy.
- Add egg and vanilla extract, and mix until well combined.
- Gradually add the dry ingredients to the butter mixture, mixing until a dough forms. The dough will be crumbly.

3. Make the Chocolate Quark Filling:

- In another bowl, beat together quark (or cream cheese), granulated sugar, egg, and vanilla extract until smooth and creamy.
- Remove about 1 cup of the mixture and stir in cocoa powder until well combined. This will be the chocolate filling.

4. Assemble the Zupfkuchen:

- Press about 2/3 of the dough into the bottom and slightly up the sides of the prepared springform pan to form a crust.
- Spread the chocolate quark filling evenly over the dough crust.
- Crumble the remaining dough over the chocolate filling. It's okay if some of the filling shows through.

5. Make the Streusel Topping:

- In a small bowl, combine granulated sugar and flour. Cut in cold cubed butter using a pastry cutter or fork until the mixture resembles coarse crumbs.
- Sprinkle the streusel topping evenly over the top of the Zupfkuchen. Optionally, sprinkle sliced almonds over the streusel.

6. Bake the Zupfkuchen:

- Bake in the preheated oven for 45-50 minutes, or until the top is golden brown and a toothpick inserted into the center comes out clean.
- Remove from the oven and let the Zupfkuchen cool in the pan on a wire rack for 15-20 minutes.

7. Serve and Enjoy:

- Once cooled slightly, release the sides of the springform pan and transfer the Zupfkuchen to a serving plate.
- Slice and serve the Zupfkuchen warm or at room temperature. It's perfect with a cup of coffee or tea.
- Store any leftovers in an airtight container in the refrigerator for up to 3 days.

This Zupfkuchen recipe combines the rich flavors of chocolate and creamy quark in a delightful marble cake form, topped with buttery streusel for added texture. Enjoy this traditional German treat for dessert or as a sweet snack!